to Pfc. Donald Swoverland
for award in the USAREUR
finals of the 1960 All Army
Photography Contest
                    by Walther Heuser

Sept. 1960
Heidelberg

More color magic with WALTHER BENSER

MORE COLOR MAGIC

with WALTHER BENSER

DR. DIENER KG. – NEUMÜNSTER

Drawings by Ursula Benser

CONTENTS

7

INDEX OF COLOR PICTURES

To My American Friends

I have written this book mainly for the carefree amateur, because here in my native Germany there is so much talk about the "deadly serious" amateur. I want to guide you through my book as a light-hearted mentor, and I hope that by the time I take leave of you I have imbued you with some of my own enthusiasm. I want to help you to grow into real amateurs, that is to say, lovers of photography in natural colors, and to enjoy with me the thrill our cameras offer day in, day out. Lastly, I want to help you to a deeper appreciation of all the beauty around us.

And you can thank your lucky stars for being amateurs. For a professional photographer must know a lot more and must busy himself to a far greater extent with technical details. And since he has to rely on his camera for his daily bread he will often find it hard to remain light-hearted, because he cannot pick up his camera just as his spirit moves him; he has to execute orders, stick to time limits, produce props and models and often follow the whims of those who pay him.

You are spared all this worry!

For you to bring home a crop of good pictures it is not essential to have a lot of theoretical knowledge. Some highly talented successful amateurs produce pictures of international fame—most of them have no clue about data tables, characteristic curves, threshold values and Kelvin degrees. I even have a well-founded suspicion that a great deal of theoretical knowledge can stand in the way of practical achievement, because it destroys that carefree innocence which is sometimes essential for success in seemingly hopeless photographic situations.

As a result of my countless contacts with photo-fans in the United States I have come to regard highly the zeal and technical knowledge with which you pursue photography in your country. I would go even further: – I am inclined to believe that phototechnical knowledge among U.S. amateurs is vaster and deeper than is generally found in Europe. In the States you have many interesting photographic periodicals, and very serious discussions go on in your clubs. In addition, excellent exposure materials are available to you in America, good color films of various brands of a high degree of color purity, def-

11

inition, and speed. And yet another difference from European conditions cannot be overlooked: – Taking photographs on color film is no luxury in the U.S., on the contrary, it is the accepted thing.

Nevertheless, there is one aim which is common to all amateurs the whole world over: – to produce good pictures, appealing not only to themselves, but also to others who were not on the spot when the pictures were taken. In spite of this urge they often neglect the best opportunities and do not progress beyond the common, or garden snapshot. The reason is almost invariably that they do not look critically and with discretion through the viewfinder of their camera, or into their finder hood.

In my slide lectures, which to date have brought me to more than a hundred cities in the U.S., I have tried to solve the problem of the snapshot, and how to improve its photographic qualities by a novel approach. Deliberately I showed my listening viewers – or viewing listeners – examples of very badly photographed pictures. I went on to demonstrate side by side the same motifs, but photographed better, in comparative projection; I believe that by this method I succeeded in leading many an amateur on to the right track. This book is meant to be a continuation and elaboration of my lectures, and to smooth the way to better color photography.

Yours truly *Walther Benser*

My Camera

Just in case you do not know yet the make of camera with which I take my pictures: – It is a Leica.

If you are already a Leica owner, holding your camera in as high esteem as I do mine, there really is no need for you to read any further because most likely you already know what I am now going to say.

I have been a Leica fan for about thirty years, and know exactly the reason why. For the translation of my photographic ideas into pictures I must have an absolutely reliable camera. I must be 100 % sure that my film lies perfectly flat in the camera, that the lenses give the best possible definition, and that their aperture ratings are not optimistic, that the focusing is pin-sharp, and the release action butter-smooth. I must be able to rely on maximum speed of action and versatility of use. I regard my Leica in much the same light as a jockey regards his best race horse. I feel like a racing driver who has hitched his ambitions to a car whose every single nut and bolt he knows and which instantly obeys the gentlest touch of his hand.

In addition to all this, I simply can no longer imagine photography without interchangeable focal lengths. A rigidly built-in lens of only a single fixed focal length would for me be a shackle which might very soon spoil all my enthusiasm for photography. It would be the same to me as a piano with only one octave to a pianist. True, he might manage – but only just – to indicate a tune on it with two fingers, but he would hardly be able to play it, full chords and all.

If you have once experienced how the limits of the angle of view of a standard lens are burst by the short focal lengths; or hitherto undreamt-of creative possibilities opened up with a tele-lens, you cannot go back any more. You will no longer be able to do without interchangeable lenses.

I must admit, though, that my enthusiasm for the Leica is of course a personal matter. Partly it stems from traditional affection and long usage. It is quite obvious that other cameras, too, are capable of producing good, even excellent, pictures.

One thing, however, is certain: – even the world's best camera does not by itself give us good photographs if we do not know how to handle it, and if the eye behind the viewfinder lacks photographic vision.

The fully-automatic camera may someday make its debut. It is the camera designers' aim to relieve the amateur of the need to think. To think? Sure, about stops and shutter speeds, depth of field and light values. The functional part is simplified, but the mental process remains.

A bell that rings when you pass a good subject will never be invented. For the decision as to what is photographically worth-while and how the subject is approached will always remain the responsibility of the photographer.

This is the point where you begin to feel the joy of being a photographer.

This joy of photography and a reliable precision camera are inseparable. This is why I am a photo-enthusiast and a Leica-fan!

How to Read this Book

This book is no thriller to be devoured from cover to cover with a sneaking look at the last page to find out "whodunnit", or whether the wedding bells are ringing.

Rather, you may browse through it as you would through a tourist guide describing in detail a place you want to see.

Also, you can leave out one chapter or another, because I am quite sure some contain information with which you are already quite familiar.

Again, there is no reason why you should not look at the pictures first, proceeding, with your interest aroused how they were taken, to a study of the commentary printed opposite.

You will notice that I have deliberately given a very broad description of each color plate, for you would derive scant benefit were I merely to give you such titles as "Profile of A Beautiful Girl". That it is a profile you will see in any case, and the beauty of the sitter is a matter of taste. In my view much more should be known about a picture: — how, when, where, and why, in what kind of light, morning, noon, or evening, and the part of the world and the season of the year in which it was taken. All this is necessary for exposure data to acquire a meaning and to be of value to the amateur.

Originally, this book was written for my amateur friends in Germany. It is therefore quite unavoidable that text and pictures should have a flavor which is, if not altogether German, at least European. I am sure that my experiences and views will not in every instance coincide with those of my friends in the U.S. But these cases, I believe, are few and far between. I think that fundamentally photographic wishes and questions are the same, and that there is no need for adapting the text to American conditions which I do not in any case claim to be familiar with in any detail.

This book sums up my experiences; it is not a photographic encyclopedia. It is meant to help you to rid yourselves of your aversion to the technical side of photography, and last, but not least, to prove that one need not be a genius to be able to produce good pictures. It takes for granted only your wish to stand out a little from the multitude of dull button-pushers.

To select one's own photographs for one's own book is a difficult task; no less difficult is it to comment on one's own pictures beyond giving the purely technical features. There always looms the danger of self-praise. You have to go a long way till you reach the point where you can view your own achievements as critically as somebody else's. Some people never manage to do this. I shall never forget someone's remark when he showed me some slides: – "This picture is not one of mine, but it is also quite good."

Memories of the First Years of the Color Film

The first color reversal films appeared on the market some 25 years ago. True, they were not the first color processes available to experienced amateurs, but the earlier films were complicated and their results not always satisfactory.

A color reversal film yields diapositives, transparent photographs, in short, transparencies. They are either mounted in cardboard frames or between glass, and enlarged on a white screen with a projector.

Provided the pictures were exposed more or less correctly, the colors will be reproduced surprisingly true-to-life. The darkened room in which we should view them often makes the projected color slide look even more luminous and colorful than we remember the original subject when it was taken.

I very clearly recall where and when I saw my first color projection. It was a memorable evening at Dr. Paul Wolff's, a man whose name is a matchless symbol to the older generation; he was one of the best-known and ablest photographers before World War II.

At that time Wolff had tried out the first Agfacolor film, with a speed rating so low that modern exposure meters no longer include it in their scales – 7° DIN, i. e. less than 6 ASA. All the same, his color slides were sensational. Most of the pictures he took with the aid of a tripod; sunlight was more or less an essential condition, and the exposure data in full sunlight and optimum lighting conditions was usually $1/10$ second at f/8.

Paul Wolff made a virtue of necessity, taking many of his subjects even then from a low camera angle against the sky, which did not as a rule have to appear sharp in the picture, at shorter shutter speeds and larger stops. Also, he concentrated much on close-up subjects and "filled his picture frames" with his subject matter, thereby avoiding a disturbing background. His technique, his particular pictorial concept, are even do-day exemplary. I consider him my great teacher.

ASA and DIN as Yardsticks for Your Exposures

Today, when we take our photographs on color films at ratings of 80 or 100 ASA without giving it much thought we must remember that this represents no less than a 25-fold increase in speed over the first color films.

The power of an automobile engine is expressed by the horse-power rating; likewise, photographic materials are described by rating values indicating their sensitivity. In the U.S.A., ASA numbers are in general use, in England BSI and Weston numbers, while European countries on the whole have adopted the DIN system. Until a short while ago, the DIN figures were expressed in /10°, which was rather tedious and confusing. Recently this has been simplified, and it is convenient to find the new, streamlined values, 14° DIN, 17° DIN, etc., translated into their ASA equivalents.

An increase of 3° DIN always represents a doubling of the speed while in the case of ASA the index number doubles along with the speed of the film.

The only snag is that all the speed ratings were originally devised for black-and-white films, and that with color films they can really only be used as a rough guide. For color films, especially reversal films, demand a vastly more accurate exposure than black-and-white films if they are to yield optimum results.

Thus, the speed ratings of color films are merely tips how to set our exposure meters. Further, the question whether our picture is dominated by light or dark colors, and particularly the way we use our exposure meter is of decisive importance. I shall return to this point in greater detail later.

The Color Film — A Photo-chemical Wonder

Without concerning ourselves overmuch with the alchemist's secrets of modern photochemistry we must appreciate that every increase in film speed raises very difficult problems which must be solved if other essential properties are not to suffer as a result of the increased sensitivity, welcome as this is. We must remember that the color film presents us not with a single emulsion, buth with three emulsions coated on top of each other.

The film makers' stroke of genius consists of their ability to coat these really extremely thin layers not only on top of each other, but above all with consistent uniformity. Nor must these emulsions ever interfere with each other during coating, storage, or processing in the developer, i. e. these three layers must never affect each other.

I think I can save myself a detailed explanation of the little miracle you trigger off as soon as you release the shutter of your camera. Since numerous text books offer enough information about this point, I would rather not bother you with the description of a subject which has no direct bearing on photo-graphic practice. We only must be sure that the color film we use in our camera is sold only after the most exacting check of each emulsion batch and that no matter where we buy it we obtain a film of as uniform characteristics as possible.

I know that this control, as strict as it is necessary, causes many thousands of feet of film to end up on the scrap heap of the plant every year.

Color Reversal or Negative Film

In color photography, two alternative ways are open to us of obtaining a reproduction in natural colors. We distinguish between two color processes, i. e.

color reversal film, and
color negative film.

With color reversal film, you simply insert the film cassette in your camera, and expose the film according to the directions enclosed or with the aid of a photo-electric exposure meter. When you have made all your exposures, you forward your film to one of the many developing stations which return the developed film to you after a few days. You then have your final color slides.

The expression "color slide", as we all know, signifies a "transparent picture in natural or near-natural tone- and color ranges". If we pass a lot of light through this transparent color picture from a projector lamp, a luminous, bright picture is produced on a white surface, the projection screen, by means of an optical system.

The real object of a color slide taken on color reversal film is its projection, apart from the possibility of viewing it through a magnifier or a so-called slide-viewer.

Color Paper Prints from Color Slides

For some time we have had facilities for making enlargements from slides on a paper or plastic base. However, experience has shown that by no means all color slides are suitable for these enlargements, not even if they project satisfactorily, if a reasonably pleasing standard is to be set for the results. For the enlarging process on paper we can in the first instance use color slides of poor contrast; the second requirement is extreme sharpness.

Color slides taken, for instance, in contrasty side- or backlighting, which are reproduced extremely well in their highlights as well as their shadows due to the great luminosity of projection, will in most cases produce a paper print which is far too harsh, with its shadows blocked, or its highlights burned out. This is simply due to the fact that the coating characteristics and the development of the color reversal film are designed exclusively for its real purpose of projection, and are therefore not generally suitable for reproduction on paper.

This perhaps over-critical approach to color photographs on paper from color slides may occasionally be refuted by one or other excellent result. Again, it may also be possible that many amateurs are not quite as critical with their own photos and are happy to have any color paper print at all. Be this as it may, the color paper enlargement from color slides does in no way stand comparison with the possibilities offered by the color negative material to be described presently. Color reversal film therefore falls very short of being a universal material for color photography.

Expensive Special Processes

Our assessment of the useful range of color slides outside projection would be incomplete without pointing out that we do in fact have methods of obtaining excellent enlargements from color reversal film. The best-known as well as the best is the Dye-Transfer Process which comes from America. This involves as a first step the production of three black-and-white color separation negatives from the original color slide. The separations are enlarged on foils or matrices of appropriate size. By the use of so-called masks the reproduction of the colors can be strongly influenced and their purity improved. The results are excellent and in every respect equal to the best enlargements from color negative film. But the cost is far greater. In the States a few years ago I offered five slides for exhibition purposes; 20 × 24″ paper enlargements were made of them by the Dye Transfer process. Thank heavens it was not I, but the exhibitors who had to foot the bill. One enlargement cost $ 100, and only further prints from the same slide were reduced to $ 25 per print. Thank you very much!

Naturally, the use of perfect color slides is very popular for reproduction purposes. After all, all the pictures in this book are exclusively based on color reversal slides. In a good printing works, where the best photo-engravers have a standing comparable to that of a first-class quarterback on a football team, color separation negatives are also made from the original slide by an extremely painstaking process. You may be interested to know that such an engraving costs between $ 150 and $ 400 depending on its size, while the outlay is no more than about $ 40 for black-and-white blocks of comparable dimensions. I am sure you realize now why books containing many color plates are so much more expensive than those with black-and-white illustrations.

Duplicate Color Slides from Color Reversal Film

The possibility of obtaining good duplicates from original color slides has improved considerably during the last few years. A great deal of experience is required, so that it will be well worth your money to leave this job to special color laboratories. The question which immediately arises as to whether the quality of such duplicates is good can be answered with yes. Certainly, a quality absolutely equal to that of the original cannot be achieved because the copying process involves a slight loss of sharpness even if reversal material is used without the introduction of an intermediate negative. Expressed in somewhat vague percentage values the sharpness amounts to about 80% of that of the original. During projection the decrease in sharpness will only be apparent if duplicate and original slide are shown side by side.

The color rendering of the duplicates is sometimes inferior to that of the originals, but in some cases it is even superior, particularly if the original had a disturbing color cast, which during the copying process could be removed through the use of appropriate filters. Inferior results invariably are the outcome of contrasty originals which during duplicating present the same difficulties that are met during enlarging on color paper: – highlights and shadows are not very readily accommodated simultaneously. Color originals poor in contrast, even a little weak ones, can, however, produce such good duplicates that even the expert will only see the difference under a magnifying glass.

Black-and-white Pictures from Color Slides

To complete my survey I must not ignore the possibility of black-and-white enlargements from color slides. Naturally, this involves a negative, with results which are often extraordinary. Their quality also depends on the extent of the brightness contrast of the color original. I for one have frequently obtained excellent black-and-white pictures from my color slides, provided the intermediate negative had been carefully exposed and meticulously developed. However, only a very small minority of amateurs will go to the trouble of doing this job themselves unless they have a great deal of practice in the development of black-and-white miniature films. The best method is the so-called optical reproduction, or projection printing, i.e. without direct contact between the slides and a black-and-white negative film.

Many photographic laboratories already treat the production of such black-and-white pictures from color slides as a matter of routine so that it is best to ask your photo-dealer to do it for you. You will then be in a position to fill your photo-album with souvenir pictures, and especially to please those whom you cannot give your color slides at least with black-and-white prints. It must be admitted, though, that the quality of such prints is somewhat inferior to that of enlargements from original black-and-white negatives, they show, under critical examination, the characteristic appearance of a reproduction, much like a print obtained from a photograph of which the negative had been lost.

What, then, is the sum total of the possibilities
of the color reversal film?

The point has been reached of reviewing once more the position of the color reversal film within the framework of color photography, since this also throws light on the discussion following below of the color negative film and its potentialities: –

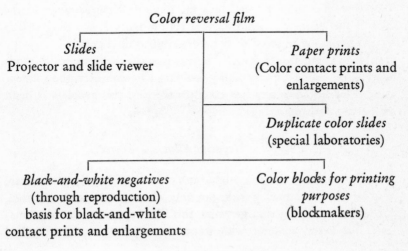

Color reversal film

Slides Projector and slide viewer	*Paper prints* (Color contact prints and enlargements)
	Duplicate color slides (special laboratories)
Black-and-white negatives (through reproduction) basis for black-and-white contact prints and enlargements	*Color blocks for printing* *purposes* (blockmakers)

23

The Color Negative Film

A negative is a reproduction which shows the light and color features of the original in reverse. This means that a white wall appears dark in a negative, and the face of a deeply sun-tanned beauty appears light. We are quite familiar with this from black-and-white photography.

But the color negative is not content with this. If, for instance, the sky above a landscape is deep blue, the color negative film will show this sky in a color which is complementary to blue, i. e. it is reproduced as its opposite, in our case a muddy orange. Green hedges, to take another example, appear reddish in our color negative.

The purpose of the color negative is the production of color prints or enlargements. The color paper used in this process is also coated with three color emulsions.

Experienced technicians in the color laboratories take great pains to achieve a color reproduction as true as possible to nature. Sometimes the author of the picture is even asked to give further details and state special wishes; for the color technician is not always in a position to know the color character of the subject accurately. With the aid of a set of various printing filters color casts are eliminated or a certain color character is introduced into the picture. Pictures taken in the light of the setting sun which have a yellow-red cast can thus, within certain limits, be restored to the more neutral daylight. It is likewise possible to eliminate the dreaded blue cast in the shadows, which spoils many a color slide with its chalky coolness. Consequently, the amateur using color negative film has no filter worries, this problem is dealt with at the darkroom stage.

The Color Negative Film is Universal

Since the people in the photo-laboratory are capable, as we have seen, of quite a lot of conjuring tricks not only concerning color corrections, but also of cropping enlargements, this film represents the ideal material for every amateur who wants to retain as much control as

24

possible over the entire photographic process from the exposure to the final picture.

We might as well admit it: – Having to bow to the necessity of sending the exposed color reversal film to a processing station is downright humiliating to someone long accustomed to developing his own black-and-white films. While the manufacturers of some color reversal films provide for the option of user-development, the centralization of processing in special laboratories appears to me to be the best solution, since the whole procedure presents too many possibilities of error in the average amateur darkroom in view of the large number of baths as well as the need for strict temperature control. Careful processing of a color reversal film in a developing tank would require about two hours, and making up all the chemicals for a single film would be far too costly. This is plain commonsense.

The situation is different in the case of color negative film. Processing is comparatively simple, even the layman – provided he adheres closely to the instructions – can obtain flawless results. Naturally, he can thereby also reduce his costs a little. However, do-it-yourself only makes sense if you do your own enlarging in addition to developing your films. Here, however, most amateurs find themselves rather restricted because they need a darkroom whose complete equipment as a color laboratory only pays if they are prepared to spend a lot of time and money on their hobby. Under these conditions the color negative film is the ideal material for their future photographic activities. For the negative provides them with prints and color enlargements of any desired part of the picture and of any size, as well as with excellent black-and-white enlargements and color slides of any number and size of outstanding quality.

In actual practice it would work out that color negative film is used exclusively for all exposures; some of the results are processed for the album, others for projection, and in the case of purely personal souvenir snaps without special color appeal for black-and-white enlargements. Filter problems hardly exist, because everything is taken care of later on in the darkroom. Also, pictorial composition at the moment of exposure can be modified to a large extent in the enlarger.

What, then, can we do with the color negative film?
Color negative
(user processing or color laboratory)

Color prints and enlargements	Color slides
	directly from the color negative

Black-and-white prints and enlargements
directly from the color negative

Which Process Suits Me Best?

At this stage of my discourse it is time to answer the often posed question whether in view of the obvious advantages of the negative film one should remain faithful to the reversal faction, or change over to the universal color negative film. Here is my view: – If your color photographs are merely meant to give you pleasure, keep fresh your memories of holidays and everyday family life, if you want to entertain your friends and relatives with an occasional slide evening of a choice of your most beautiful color photographs in your own home, there is no reason why you should not stick to the color reversal film. The single outlay of a small home projector is the cheapest and simplest means of deriving complete satisfaction from your hobby; because it is beyond all argument that no technique, however ingenious, of color paper enlarging equals, let alone surpasses, the luminosity and beauty of the colors in projected transparencies.

As you buy your color reversal film you already pay for a large part of the whole process, mounting your slides between glass costs more time than money, and you are relieved of your worries about perfect development by your processing station.

When your color film is returned from processing you know at once which pictures have turned out well. Although wrong exposures and other mistakes are annoying, you will learn from them and do better next time. Possibly the film will have been returned from development so quickly that the spoiled pictures can be repeated. Occasional wishes for album prints in color as well as black-and-white can be satisfied under certain conditions.

The color negative film appeals more to the amateur with little or no interest in the projection of his photographs who prefers to have his

pictures more or less enlarged. Color paper prints can be tucked away in your wallet or stuck in an album, to be shown any time of the day or night. They can be sent away or given as presents. One does not readily part with a good color reversal slide, while any number of copies can be made from a negative film. The most beautiful or amusing photograph of your youngest, or a pretty family group easily goes in the envelope addressed to the grandparents who, presbyopic as they probably are, would not know what to do with the tiny color slide.

Amateurs who occasionally want to ride their hobby-horse for professional purposes will prefer color enlargements: architects show the beauty of their buildings harmonizing with the surrounding landscape, horticulturalists their flower beds and gardens, textile designers the latest fashion trends. The possibilities of using the hobby of color photography for profit are so numerous that it is futile even to try to cover them all.

The answer to the question whether you will be converted to "color negativism" you can now supply yourselves. It is, above all, a question of money and also of your aims in photography. Whatever your decision may be, the time has now come to deal in more detail with problems peculiar to the color negative film.

How are Color Negatives Chosen?

In complete contrast with the color reversal film, the negative film fresh from development is not at all easy to judge. Nobody shares our joy over successful exposures because hardly anyone has any idea about the reproduction of the complementary colors. Are we not ourselves a little puzzled with our photographic creations? The uncertainty whether or not the exposures are a success in their color harmony is far greater than during the judgment of black-and-white films.

Some much-to-be-envied connoisseurs with a vast store of darkroom experience can very quickly assess the enlarging qualities when examining color negatives, uttering appreciative grunts with certain exposures.

27

They remind me of the conductor who, a sheaf of music tucked under his arm, disappeared into the silence of a deep forest, to return home after some time with tears in his eyes because reading the score had touched him so profoundly.

Since it is difficult to judge the complementary-colored negatives at first glance, small color enlargements should first be made of all exposures whose sharpness is beyond suspicion and which are otherwise promising. $^{1}/_{20}$–$^{6}/_{20}$ size is quite satisfactory. Cheaper is a contact print of the entire film on paper strips or a large 8 × 10″ sheet which is of particular advantage if all the frames had received a uniformly good exposure. Otherwise, obviously only the correctly-exposed frames will appear in satisfactory colors on these contact prints. Such contacts provide, with the aid of a magnifying glass, a quite reliable means of assessment.

The very best photographs are then selected for larger formats. Larger in this context means at least $3^{1}/_{4}$ × $4^{1}/_{4}$ or 4 × 6″ size. Of course, 5 × 7 or 8 × 10″ are better still.

Altogether, the success of a color photograph on paper is governed completely by its size. In the $^{1}/_{20}$–$^{6}/_{20}$ format how insignificant and unimpressive do we find even a master shot – and how forcefully are we affected by a strong enlargement! When on the occasion of the 1958 Cologne Photokina I was asked by some photographic manufacturers to submit some color prints from negatives to be selected for large-size photographs I entered 10 color prints in postcard size, only to have the lot of them returned to me with a courteous note. That was a blow!

Whereupon I made a critical selection and, money no object, had three pictures blown up to the considerably more imposing 10 × 12″ size, which I resubmitted. Result: – "Why didn't you send us these pictures in the first place, we want two of them at once, please let us have the negatives by return of post!"

Giant Prints from Miniature Negatives

Serious Leica amateurs, the so-called sharpshooters among photographers, had until recently no more than a pitying smile whenever the miniature negative color film cropped up in a discussion. It must be admitted that initially films available for the Leica left much to be desired in the way of definition, and their graininess cannot be compared with the fine grain of present-day thin-emulsion black-and-white films. Strict limitations were therefore imposed on color enlargements, and prints beyond 8 × 10″ could hardly be viewed close-up without provoking critical comments on a certain breaking-up of image contours.

Only a few years ago this situation seemed to represent a final stage beyond which no further progress was possible; three color emulsions, no matter how thinly coated, apparently raised insoluble problems.

I know many Leica enthusiasts who did not want to do without the negative/positive process going to the length of buying a second, large-size camera.

In addition to the two processes offered by Eastman Kodak, Kodacolor and Ektacolor, Agfa surprised the amateurs with new miniature films, first CN 17, followed by CN 14 (CN stands for Color Negative, the number indicates the DIN speed rating).

Obviously, since any increase in speed results in an increase in grain size, the relatively slow 14° DIN film (CN 14) is preferable whenever satisfactory lighting conditions permit. It is – believe it or not – possible to blow up a sharp and correctly exposed miniature negative on CN 14 to sizes of 3 ft. and larger; its definition and fineness of grain compares favorably with any black-and-white enlargement of similar proportions, even under close scrutiny.

How is the Color Negative Film Exposed?

I shall presently go into the question of exposure methods for color reversal film at great length. I shall do this in the most detailed manner, not only because I am conscious of the fact that by far the greatest section of my readers use color reversal film, but also because to obtain a good color slide the exposure of such films must be particularly critical.

Clearly a color negative, too, needs the best possible exposure, although this process offers a somewhat greater latitude since certain lapses can still be made good during the enlarging stage.

When exposing color negative films as distinct from reversal films the shadows and/or the darker portions of the picture must be given prime consideration. This is why the negative film, even though it is rated at 40 ASA, appears slower compared with the 50 ASA reversal film than the difference in the speed values would indicate. In fact, experience shows that for the same subject CN 17 requires 75% more exposure than CT 18 (reversal) film which should be exposed mainly for the brightest picture areas. Nevertheless, there is no reason why you should not set your exposure meter at 40 ASA (or 20 ASA with CN 14), but you would be well advised to take your reading from the dark picture portions and, whenever you have any doubt, give a little more generous exposure. There is, moreover, an exposure table enclosed with every color negative film which offers quite reliable and useful directions to start with.

Color Slides Direct from Color Negative Film

At first glance it would appear that color slides made from color negative originals have great advantages over the reversal slide because of the possibility for subsequent control of color characteristics, as well as the facility for cropping and enlarging. As soon as the film specially designed for such copying purposes is ready for the market this question may possibly be answerable in the affirmative. At the present stage, however, I still prefer – quite apart from the question of cost – the original slide on reversal film to that drawn from a negative film. The current quality of color slides printed from color negatives corresponds roughly with that of direct duplicates from original slides, with the difference that the latter are not in all cases really satisfactory (especially in case of flat subjects), while a print from the negative offers wider latitude and control.

If you are especially interested in the mass production of slide copies you would be well advised to follow the publications in the photographic press, since at the moment everything is still very much in a state of flux.

The Exposure

On the preceding pages I have already given you some basic tips about the exposure of color film. We have learnt that in the case of reversal films – of prime interest to us here – it must be very critical if only because corrections at a later stage are, if at all, only possible within very confined limits.

Simple Exposure Tables are not Bad

If your photo-dealer advises you to use a good photo-electric exposure meter for your color films he will be right even if your black-and-white exposures of the past had been almost faultless. In this context it is interesting to note that according to statistics a high percentage of all common-or-garden amateur pictures are exposed within a range producing acceptable results. A much larger percentage of pictures suffers from other faults, such as camera shake, wrong focusing, etc.

For the run-of-the-mill color pictures, i.e. those taken during the summer under favorable lighting conditions, an exposure table offering no more than rough guidance can be completely satisfactory. Cartons of color film of every make contain instructions for their use giving valuable hints for your exposures. They are also an aid if you have accidentally left your exposure meter at home. Furthermore, the exposure table is very welcome for correction where the photo-electric meter reading is wide of the mark. If for people outdoors it does not give you data very similar to those indicated by the table, either something must be wrong with your meter, or you have taken a faulty reading for which you must find the reason. The exposure tables are efficient so long as we take our photographs under uniform, easily classifiable lighting conditions, when, to make matters easier still, the so-called exposure latitude of the color reversal film will be larger than is generally assumed.

During the summer, on the beach for instance, you may with the sun in a favorable position take the same subject at

$$f/8 \quad \text{and} \quad 1/250 \text{ second}$$
$$f/5.6 \quad \text{and} \quad 1/250 \text{ second}$$
$$f/4 \quad \text{and} \quad 1/250 \text{ second}$$

CHILDREN ON THE BEACH

A picture out of a series of at least a dozen, all of which were successful. If I only knew the mother of these two so absorbed in their play in the North Sea resort of Langeoog! I could give her a lot of pleasure with some of the color transparencies! This was a case where the camera had to follow the children unconditionally. They are still too young to pose, and after a few curious glances at the picture-taking uncle completely ignored the Leica. The large rubber duck and the ball are much more important.

Unless you pre-arrange your children's pictures on the beach you have to be content with the surroundings as you find them. A crowded beach is not ideal, because the background is a-crawl with colors and contours. However, the closer we take children at play and the more deliberately we avoid all disturbing details by a clever direction of our camera the more concentrated will the final picture be. In this example I therefore made a point of eliminating the horizon and any unnecessary surroundings.

I also benefited from the greater speed of the Agfacolor film. In the late afternoon, the normal exposure time on the beach was $^1/_{100}$ second at f/8. However, I chose the shorter shutter speed of $^1/_{250}$ second in order to avoid movement blur even at close quarters. The iris, with a little push, was set just beyond f/5.6 and kept at this setting irrespective of front, side, or back light.

Leica, 50 mm. Summicron, about f/5.6, $^1/_{250}$ second, sunlight, August, about 4 p. m.

AMONG THE SAND DUNES

Aren't you surprised, dear reader? Have you ever seen such tame sea-gulls? The secret is sandwiches! Of course, the scene was rehearsed, and the approach of the seagull was carefully prepared. We held the bait always in one direction, and it cost us more than one sandwich!

However, Emma, the gull, makes up for it by performing like a circus artiste. Isn't it wonderful the way her white plumage stands out against the blue sky? One almost thinks one can touch the soft coat of feathers, everything is modelled so clearly.

In order to place the figures as clearly as possible against the calm backdrop of the sky, I went down on my haunches a little. With color film this is almost more important than with black-and-white film. Although here quite a number of different colors play their part, every-one of them now has an effect of its own, because each is all at once isolated and blended by the neutral tints of sand and sky.

Lighting conditions on the beach are ideal! The tenuous haze of cirrus cloud subdues the blue radiation, and the bright beach reflects the light in all directions. Thus the purity of the colors is preserved even in the most delicate shadows.

Leica, 50 mm. Summicron, between f/5.6 and f/8, $^1/_{250}$ second, August, sunlight, about 2 p. m.

(with, say, a color film of 32 ASA). None of these pictures will be completely spoiled, although you varied your stop through two full values. It is true that the first picture may turn out rather dark due to the rather short exposure it had, the sky appearing dark blue and the other colors excessively saturated, but its projecting quality might be quite acceptable. The third picture will look very much brighter, perhaps some detail will have been lost in the white sand, but it may not be a total loss. The second picture is probably just right. This example shows you that motifs with small contrast range, completely illuminated in the shadows and probably receiving additional reflected light from all directions, may have a practical exposure latitude of 2 stop values. This, though, is the most favorable case we come across in practice. If we confined ourselves to such situations we would be able to do without any exposure meter altogether.

However, exposure latitude shrinks as soon as lighting contrasts rise with side- or back lighting, or when objects with colors of different brightness values are involved. Here, a variation within one stop will change the result considerably.

The Chaos of Numbers

I have learned from my own lectures not to expect my audience to be as familiar with the concept of aperture stops and shutter speeds as

somebody to whom this has become second nature through long years of practice.

If you have used your camera for a long time, you will not be puzzled any more by the series of stop numbers 2.8, 4, 5.6, 8, 11, 16, etc. You will simply know that f/8 transmits less light through the lens than, say, f/5.6, let alone f/4. But maybe you do not know that these numbers are mutilated fractions, with the numerator omitted from the engraved scale for lack of space.

That $1/8$ lb. of coffee is less than $1/4$ lb. is a fact that we in Europe are acutely conscious of from a time we prefer not to remember. That f/8 (i.e. $1/8$) transmits less light than f/4 ($1/4$), puzzles some otherwise highly respectable and intelligent people, well able to hold their own in the day-to-day struggle that is life. And thus it passes at times that someone trying to follow the advice of giving a longer exposure turns his stop in all good faith on to a higher number achieving the very opposite effect.

The shutter speeds represent a second pitfall for beginners. Here, too, if the confusion of numbers is not to be worse confounded it is quite impossible to register all the fractions as $1/60$, $1/125$, $1/250$ second etc., so that for reasons of clarity the sequence is often given as 60, 125, 250 etc.

The prevailing chaos is further increased because some cameras have a different shutter sequence, some older models even different aperture stop scales (4.5, 6.3, 9, 12.5 etc.). However, efforts are now made to achieve uniformity in most cameras also in the shutter speed scales, so that with the variation of the exposure time the speed is, where possible, exactly halved or doubled. My own Leica still has the old division of $1/25$, $1/50$, $1/100$, $1/250$ second, but current models have switched over to the geometric progression which permits a more even spacing of exposure times. It now reads: – 1, $1/2$, $1/4$, $1/8$, $1/15$, $1/30$, $1/60$, $1/125$, $1/250$, $1/500$ and $1/1000$ second.

The fact that the technical data of my pictures are still based on the old scale division should not concern the reader whose camera is calibrated differently. In practice, $1/50$ and $1/60$ second, or $1/100$ and $1/125$ second lie so close together as to make no difference.

It is much more important to know that a decrease in the stop naturally calls for an increase in the exposure time. If you have found that the time recommended by your table or exposure meter is $1/25$ second at f/8, you must be aware that if you increase your exposure time to $1/60$ second, you must stop your diaphragm down to f/11, and at $1/30$ second to f/16 in order to maintain the same amount of exposure. With a simple Box Brownie these worries do not exist because its lens generally works at a fixed aperture of f/14, and the appropriate shutter speed of about $1/40$ second is also fixed. However, satisfactory results can only be expected under optimum conditions of lighting.

Is the Light Value System a Solution?

There are cases without number in which amateurs who took the step from a Box Brownie to a more expensive camera brought home pictures inferior to those they had made with the simpler camera. They stumbled over the extended possibilities and were confused about the shutter-speed/lens-stop relationship. This led to the introduction of the "light-value", whose usefulness in actual practice is, however, extremely debatable.

A situation has now been reached where many modern exposure meters not only indicate stop numbers and shutter speeds, but an additional, third series of numbers, those of the light values. Shutters bearing these numbers are set a the light value after measurement, when they automatically set the appropriate stop. But this very practical simplification based on coupling shutter speed and stop number has one snag. It does not cover by a long chalk the entire range of exposures. True, this range varies from one camera model to the next; however, in all of them the automatic coupling must at once be disengaged if the light value mechanism can no longer function, in the face of special depth-of-field problems or when fast lenses are used at full aperture. Every advanced worker therefore considers the light value setting in its present form more a hindrance than a help because it makes the individual approach to exposure problems more difficult.

Hence, the light value is really of use only to those amateurs who stay within the range of "fair-weather photography" and do not wish to run the risk when they occasionally change their exposure time of forgetting the attendant change of their stop setting. This reminds me of a charming example: –

Outside a small photo-dealers' at a North Sea resort, on the way to the beach, we found a blackboard on which were chalked the words
"Today my customers use light value 14".

The man knew his customers. The weather was fair, no cloud darkened the sky, and the same lighting conditions could absolutely be counted upon the livelong day.

A glance at the table or the meter showed that the indicated light value 14 meant f/16 and $1/60$ second, or f/11 and $1/125$ second, or f/8 and $1/250$ second. Here, the indication of the light value number pure and simple offered an advantage because everybody could choose for himself the shutter-speed/stop combination he liked without the risk of wrong exposure. The children playing ball among the sand dunes could obviously be taken best with a short shutter speed such as $1/250$ second, while the family blissfully relaxing in the sand needed more depth of field (from the tip of the toe to the lighthouse in the background), i.e. a smaller stop involving a longer exposure time.

The photo-electric exposure meter

Many years ago, before there was any widespread amateur color photography, we already had measuring instruments to enable us to determine our exposures more accurately. They consisted of kaleidoscope-like little tubes through which the subject was viewed. Inside one saw round, numbered little windows, in circular arrangement, which became progressively darker. And according to whether the subject was lighter or darker, the number in the little window, 9 or 11 or even 13, could only just be recognized. On a table outside, the shutter speed and stop corresponding to the number shown in the little window was read off. Although a little cumbersome, the method was quite useful in its application as long as the photographer's eyesight was not playing him any tricks.

Today we have photo-electric exposure meters. They make use of light-sensitive cells able to convert light energy into an electric current of minute strength but sufficient to move a small meter pointer. As soon, then, as the meter shows a reading, stop and shutter-speed or the appropriate exposure value is read off. Obviously, the film speed must have been set beforehand on the instrument.

My wholehearted admiration is due to these exposure meters. The way they are used, and their reaction to minute light differences reminds me of divining rods with which dowsers find hidden water.

It is difficult to say which of the multitude of exposure meters is the best. If possible, its angle of acceptance should not be too large and its cell should measure the colors correctly, i.e. it should not only register light and dark, but also differences in the brightness values of the colours. Among the modern top-class instruments, of which there are about a dozen on the market, all fulfil this demand as far as I am aware. However, the measuring accuracy of the instrument largely depends on how we use it.

But once we are familiar with the way it functions, the assistance of the exposure meter will become little short of indispensable. It is an established fact that even an expensive exposure meter will soon pay for itself, since it greatly reduces the number of faulty exposures.

Which Exposure Meter?

My answer to this question is quite simple: – "The one that you are used to." In fact, the knowledge of the characteristics of a measuring instrument to which one is used, and with whose snags one is familiar, is more important than anything else. The question as to whether it is better to work with an exposure meter built into the camera (electric eye camera) rather than with a separate instrument may briefly be answered thus: Most built-in exposure meters have a smaller measuring range than those that are carried in the pocket. This is quite a natural consequence because building the meter into the camera calls for the greatest possible reduction in size. There is the further disadvantage that in most cases whenever the meter has to be repaired the camera has to be sent along with it. Should the camera be dropped – which does happen upon occasion – both will be ruined if the worst comes to the worst. Futhermore, the meter will often have to be used from a position other than that of the camera.

The Leicameter M-c sits piggyback-fashion on top of the Leica – an ideal solution, because it can be removed at a single stroke in spite of the fact that it is coupled semi-automatically with the Leica's shutter-speed dial. Nevertheless, I also like to use a meter which can not only be carried round the neck, but also hidden under the jacket. In photo-graphically "under-developed" countries my camera invariably attracts swarms of children and teenagers (Sicily, Spain, Greece, Turkey, etc.). If I worked with a built-in or a push-on exposure meter, I would have difficulty in camouflaging my photographic intentions. However, with a meter worn round my neck I am able to determine my exposure reading without betraying my real intentions. The subsequent snapshot will then merely be a matter of seconds.

Naturally, our eyes react with far greater sensitivity to light than does any electric measuring instrument. In twilight we can still recognize detail when the meter has long "gone to sleep". Nevertheless, we are more easily subject to illusions when light and dark change rapidly. If we move into bright sunlight from a dimly-lit room, we will at first be strongly dazzled, and see the light brighter than a few minutes later. We recognize this adaptability of the eye even more clearly on entering a darkroom where highly sensitive photographic material is processed. The girls' cheerful chatter, the clatter of dishes and enlargers indicate that everyone is hard at work here. To our eyes, however, everything seems shrouded in darkness at first. Gradually, details will appear out of the gloom while the eyes become adapted.

It is therefore understandable that we are the worst possible judges of small differences in exposure, even if our experience will in time give us more reliable results. Although I am now able to expose with some assurance even without measuring instruments, I'd much rather consult my light meter almost before every new setting, gratefully accepting its small corrections. We have become inseparable.

Later on, I shall explain with a few examples how to handle an exposure meter so that only the really important light is measured. But first of all we want to make ourselves familiar with the instrument.

The exposure meter is put to the test

Whether Sixtomat, or Leicameter, Weston Master, Lucimeter, or any other instrument, every meter should serve its master as faithfully as possible. However, for this purpose we must really put it through its paces as thoroughly as we can, because an exposure meter, set in good faith at a certain film speed, can spoil the enjoyment of our whole holiday if out of sheer cussedness it gives excessively long or short readings.

Here is my method of calibrating exposure meter, camera, and color film with each other.

First of all, we set our meter at the recommended speed setting of the film used (50 ASA for example), and look for the ideal average subject in full sunlight. This is particularly easy during the summer half of the year between 10 and 11 a.m. or between 1 and 2 p.m. (When your own shadow is a little longer than yourself is the right time to look for your subject.)

By average subject we mean one containing light as well as dark colors. This is easier said than found. Mary nextdoor, true enough, wears dark drainpipe jeans, a sweater with red and yellow stripes, and has a light complexion; all this would make her the ideal average subject. But if we placed her in front of a dark green hedge, this would influence the meter reading more than it should. Likewise, a light wall would be unsuitable as background for Mary's colorful display, because it would reflect too much light, therefore also falsifying the reading.

The ideal average subject

The best suggestion I could think of would therefore be a very gaudy billboard. This does not move, makes no fuss, while offering a rich scale of colors. If it is in the centre of the picture, part of the back-

ground can be light, part dark, and this will not unduly influence the reading; it shows up all the better the differential color reproduction of our test series.

However, we must take care to avoid an excess of white areas in the sign as well as in the background.

We now approach to within about 7 feet of our subject without measuring our own shadow, and take a meter reading. Let us assume – this was the case in my own test – the result to be f/8 and $^1/_{100}$ second. This will then be our initial exposure, around which we shall build a test-exposure sequence.

Now is the time to get hold of a notebook and to record our data. This is much better than relying on one's memory. Now we press the button, having set the correct distance (quite important, this!). The picture is best taken with the camera held horizontally, and with a standard focal length lens the exposure distance will be just right at about 13 feet.

We are now set to start our exposure series. The next exposure is, of course, made without any change of the shutter speed of $^1/_{100}$ second, at half a stop smaller, i. e. instead of f/8 halfway between f/8 and f/11. The third exposure takes place at a further half stop down, i. e. f/11, and if we want to make our test particularly convincing, a further one or two pictures, at half a stop smaller each, would supply us with certain under-exposures.

The same procedure is now repeated in the other direction, that of longer exposures, by first using, for example, between f/8 and f/5.6, then proceeding to f/5.6, between f/5.6 and f/4, f/4, and perhaps even between f/4 and f/2.8. If by now we have not yet made any notes, it is our last chance!

By the way, a thing I quite forgot to mention – unfortunately, we would have to repeat the entire series if in the meantime the sun had disappeared behind a cloud, and we had not patiently awaited its full return.

In order to get our results as quickly as possible, we had better make haste to expose the remainder of our film. The standard exposure table enclosed with every film will give us sufficient guidance to enable us to add this or that color picture even without complete confidence in our exposure meter. But, here, too, we should never fail to make notes of our exposure data, covering not only stop and shutter speed, but also time of day and the position of the sun.

Correct assessment of the test series

As soon as the film has come back from the processing station, we have to arrange for it to be viewed under favorable conditions by transmitted light. A piece of white paper on a bright, if possible sunlit, windowsill will help us to find the ideally-exposed picture quickly by comparing it with the others. If the first, initial exposure corresponds most closely to the colors present when the picture was taken, we can trust our exposure meter henceforth at 50 ASA. If it is the next exposure, we must either use it at the next larger or next smaller ASA number. I know instruments which have to be set up to 100 ASA, but work very reliably on this basis.

During this adjustment it is brought home to us how important our notes during the exposures were. It is to be hoped they were not jotted on the back of a cigarette box or envelope! I speak from my own experience!

Incidentally, it is a good idea to pore over our test strips together with our photo dealer. He will most probably make use of a magnifying glass and has perhaps more experience than we have, in order to arrive at the correct conclusions from the test strip.

The tolerance

I would not like to conclude this chapter on the calibration of the exposure with camera and color film without taking the opportunity of clearing up a widely held error. Addicts of photography generally speak of correct and faulty indications of exposure meters. The instrument is held responsible for errors which frequently have their cause elsewhere.

Not so long ago, a friend of mine complained "Three times now I have sent my meter to the factory", and asked me to put a word in for him with the makers on his fourth attempt. I did have a few doubts about this thrice-repeated failure of putting things right. I asked for his camera and had its shutter tested by a camera mechanic; the shutter speeds turned out to be considerably shorter than the values engraved on the shutter speed dial. $1/50$ second, his most frequently used exposure time, was almost $1/100$ second. Small wonder, then, that the marriage between camera and exposure meter was not a very happy one!

If we went to the trouble of testing our cameras for the reliability of their shutter speeds and our lenses for the trustworthiness of their relative apertures – we should have the surprise of our lives! Far be it from me to make general statements about all cameras being inaccurate and lenses being slower than they rashly claim to be. All the same, some of them allow for tolerances which are quite considerable.

I can completely and truly vouch for the Leica and its lenses. I know the painstakingly accurate testing methods employed in the Wetzlar works. They are one of the reasons why Leitz does not build any "cheap cameras". And also one of the main reasons why I have been such a confirmed Leica man for 30 years. I must have the feeling of absolute reliability of my photographic equipment when I raise my camera to my eyes.

Let us sum up. The test sequence is not only a cross-check of the exposure meter, but it also supplies us with knowledge of the relationship between lighting conditions, camera and color film at a given reading of the measuring instrument.

How to view color transparencies

Quite deliberately I persuaded you during the exposure test in front of the billboard to expend your color film quite ruthlessly. Quite deliberately, too, I led you into the regions of under- and over-exposure through the steps of half-stop values in both directions. It was, from the beginning, fairly safe to assume that the correct exposure would

lie at about f/8 or perhaps between f/5.6 and f/8 at $^1/_{100}$ second. Would it not therefore have been quite unnecessary to make exposure tests down to f/11 and smaller, and up to f/4 and larger?

As we should expect, a first glance at the test strip already reveals how the colors "misbehave" in both directions.

But please do not throw your test strip and notes away yet, not even when you have finally determined the speed rating at which your meter should be set in future. For now you can at your complete leisure and convenience study the appearance of the colors under various exposure conditions. You will find that their reaction to generous or short exposure is not uniform!

Blue sky is the worst possible light source in which to view color transparencies, because it obviously displaces all color values a little towards blue. This impairs our objective judgment. As I have already said, a light windowsill is more suitable, particularly when the sun is shining on it.

I built my own little viewing table at home with U-shaped daylight fluorescent tubes under opal glass. The effective color temperature measured at the viewing table is 5.800° K, i.e. it very closely corresponds to the average value of white sunlight.

On my travels I view my transparencies against an office lamp screened by a sheet of white copying paper. However, my most exquisite pleasure – surpassing even that of reading a crime thriller – is with such a paper fixed in front of the bedside lamp or bedlamp, like a little curtain with a pin, looking at one transparency after another thoroughly in this bright light before dropping off to sleep.

Colors show different reactions

Returning to your test strip, you will note first of all that the "whites" will have withstood the rigors of the exposure series best of all. Naturally in the darkest transparency they will appear rather muddy, but least affected of all colors. Bright yellow, bright red, but pink and orange, too, still behave reasonably well in the shorter exposure ranges. On the other hand, the darker colors show a far more pronounced loss of luminosity. Dark blue, dark red, and especially dark green are more or less swallowed up, and are turned into black, losing much of their character. If now you compare with a quick glance the definitely overexposed pictures with the correct transparency, it will strike you that the very light photographs will have a decidedly unpleasant color character. (This becomes particularly noticeable in the sky, of which, I hope, nothing at all or only very little appears in your test picture!) Even the colors of those test pictures that have not been totally overexposed, which could be described merely as generously exposed, are weaker than necessary, compared with the "right" transparency.

Turning now to the shorter exposures in the immediate neighborhood of the pictures judged to be correct, you will, it is true, find a slight muddiness of the darker colors, however, the lighter tones show a brilliance greatly preferable to the washed-out appearance of the generous exposures.

These transparencies, which the expert describes as short-, but not under-exposures, are eminently suitable for projection, particularly if a crystal bead screen is used.

I do hope you understand me correctly. This test is not a recommendation to expose your color pictures on the short side on principle. The correct exposure has been, is, and always will be, the best. However, practice has shown that pictures of a somewhat short exposure give us more pleasure than those of a more generous exposure.

In my experience, by the way, most color transparencies are on average a little overexposed. Nevertheless, the amateurs are quite happy, because they are unaware that a shorter exposure would have given still better results.

In spite of my pleasure in the higher speed of reversal film I already have a notion that this tendency, this trend towards generous exposure, may possibly be the cause of much disappointment at first.

Perhaps you might think the following remark superfluous, but often the terms of under-exposure and over-exposure are confused within the context of color film. This is due to the fact that for ages past we have described light, thin, black-and-white negatives as "under" and dark ones as "over". In contrast to this, of course, the exact opposite is true of the reversal film. Here, the light, thin transparencies are overexposed, and the dark, muddy ones underexposed. I want to make a point of committing this to print once again, because amateurs so frequently complain to me after my lectures, telling me that their own pictures did not have remotely as beautiful and luminous colors as my own, because they had all been underexposed. Even without seeing the evidence, a few questions are enough to convince me that they mean light, thin, i.e. overexposed color transparencies.

Only one ideal exposure?

The answer to this question can be "Yes" or "No" according to the subject and its illumination. With subjects of great contrast, with very light and very dark color tones, only one extremely precise exposure time will produce the maximum of correct color reproduction. This is particularly true of subjects in side light, and even more so, in *contrejour* lighting.

Let me give you the often-quoted example of bride and bridegroom in front of the church door. He in black, she in shining white, with a huge bunch of roses in her hand, and the whole group perhaps lit from one side. In spite of all my experience, I would not be able to manage with a single exposure on such an occasion. The old "shot-gun" method with several different stops would appear to me to be the best means of finding the ideal exposure. (Perhaps you would do well in this connection to read the caption of the picture of the Concordia Temple at Agrigento on page 19 where the thousand-year-old shady olive tree presented me with pretty exposure problems.)

On the other hand, where the color contrasts are small and the illumination even (I would again give the cover picture, and the photographs on pp 27 & 101 as examples) things will be easy. Acceptable results will be obtained on either side of the ideal exposure, so that in order to get a satisfactory picture one does not necessarily have to resort to taking several exposures.

Little wonder, then, that in every elementary guide book to color photography front lighting is recommended in order to make the first steps easier for the beginner. With the sun in his back he walks on a wide, safe road, and because the greater exposure latitude largely compensates for errors, neither too little, nor too much will land him in the ditch right away. You should therefore accept this rule without question for your first color film, and, to begin with, leave those subjects alone whose strong contrasts will present too difficult a task for you.

However, it will not be long before the novice becomes fed up with the pictures showing faces and groups in dazzling sunlight, with everybody shielding their eyes with their hands in order to manage some friendly smiles for the camera. The town hall front, the monument on the market square, the plump flower girl, surrounded by her colorful display, one's own house with garden and rose bushes, all this has been taken in full sunlight, and the results are satisfying.

But even the enthusiastic acclaim of your whole family and friends greeting your first color-photographic creations should not blind you to the fact that the real task lies still in wait for you. Thus the day arrives on which you want to set your sights higher. This, though, will hardly be possible without an exposure meter which is used accurately. But if you have not studied its operating instructions closely before you use it, you may possibly make more mistakes with the exposure meter than if you had continued to rely on the simple table. Nor does this take into account the calibration by the test exposure series described on page 43/44.

VENICE

An example how in photography, too, the rule "Pars pro toto" can be applied to advantage. It means roughly "representation of a typical part in place of the whole thing". Often it expresses the essence of a subject more poignantly.

Only a strip of this proud and picturesque architecture, more hinted at than seen in the background, is enough. The reflection of the palazzo grows into the reflected blueness of the Adriatic sky.

Here, too, the symbols of this city, the black gondolas, dominate the stagnant water of the lagoon as sombre ornaments – redoubled and enlarged by the reflections.

I must mention as a technical point that for this "shot into the water" I needed a longer exposure time than for a comparable direct view of the sun-lit canal front.

With this deliberate direction of the camera towards the water, the problem is solved of bridging such a large contrast range as exists between "top" and "bottom". The – unavoidable – over-exposure of the narrow strip across the top is not harmful. Naturally, the gondalas had to be at least suggested in the original; the black reflection alone might perhaps have produced an interesting puzzle picture but not a convincing picture of Venice.

Again, the wide-angle lens was necessary in order to cover from a close range the largest possible expanse of water reflecting the sky.

Leica, 35 mm. Summaron, between f/5.6 and f/8, $^{1}/_{50}$ second, September, 2 p. m.

50

SIESTA

*Everyone who has been to Venice knows the meaning of this picture.
The gondolieri are having their siesta on the Piazetta in front of the
Palace of the Doges. Every day at noon you can see them sitting there,
lazily stretching themselves, with their feet up comfortably on empty
chairs, busy with their fingernails or just having a peaceful nap. The
very essence of Dolce Far Niente!*

*All this is enacted in the narrow strip of shadow cast by one of the
two famous columns. Every five minutes, the row of sleepers stirs,
because the shadow moves on, and one must follow it across the
square.*

*I was very keen on a picture of this scene alone, which is so typical of
Venice. However, from a normal viewpoint I would never have been
able to isolate the group from the crowds on the Piazetta and the restless background. I therefore mounted the five or six steps of the
base of the column, stood on my toes to gain the last inch of height,
when I just succeeded in getting this group of eight men diagonally on
my film. Thus the shadow of the column, too, played its humourously
illustrative part.*

*It is advisable to operate without much fuss and to get your pictures
quickly, because it would be a pity if the natural and relaxed pose of
the Gondolieri were spoiled by attracting their attention. But as you
see, I was lucky. None of them noticed me, and I was able to capture
the sleepy atmosphere prevailing at the height of a southern day.*

Leica, 50 mm. Summicron, f/11, $1/50$ second, sunlight, about 1 p.m.

A little while ago, I met a young married couple. They told me how photography had brought them together.

During a business trip in Southern Germany he used a short wait between train connections to stretch his legs on the station square. It happened to be a bright sun-drenched day after freshly fallen snow, and the nearby mountains were bathed in wonderful light. On the square in front of the railway station he watched a group of young girl students, who, chattering and giggling, formed themselves into a "picture", while one of them endeavoured, at the appropriate distance, to bring order into the confusion through her camera viewfinder. He fell for her, head over heels, immediately.

Since he was an "advanced amateur", his second glance told him that in all likelihood the picture would be a failure. The group had formed in *contre-jour* light, and the sun which was rather low above the horizon sent its light straight into the camera lens, which was devoid of any lens hood. He was sorely tempted to walk up to her courteously, raise his hat and, as a thoughtful gesture, hold it above the camera to shield it from the sun's rays, but he decided against this form of approach, which, no matter how plausible it might perhaps be, would nevertheless look a little ridiculous.

However, the ice was broken when the charming young lady tried to consult her exposure meter. It happened to be the very same type as he used. Pointing the measuring window from the camera towards the group, unaware of the bombardment by the sun's rays and the reflecting snow all around her, she was just about to transfer the obviously wrong reading to her camera. He took his courage in both hands and stepped in. Although his voice nearly failed him at the look she gave him he remarked, in as matter-of-fact a tone as he could manage: "This can't possibly turn out well!" Whereupon he gently took the exposure meter from her hand, taking her, with avuncular care and soft pressure, by the arm. He took her, the exposure meter always close in front of her eyes, step by step towards the group. At first the pointer showed a very strong deflection towards the right, but when the meter was tilted towards the legs of the giggling girls, it already began to swing back a little. Finally, at a distance of about 3 feet, the needle stopped at the f/5.6 indicated by the measuring cross.

"Well", said the young man, "there's your stop – or did you want to get your faces pitch black against the mountains?" The absence of the lens hood then provided enough material to continue the conversation. He showed his trick with the hat and its shadow, and since in his opinion she released her shutter far too abruptly at $1/100$ second, the photographic lesson was well under way.

Finally, she joined the group, while he replaced in person the missing self-timer. A theatrically exaggerated viewpoint, which photograph-ically placed the group against the sky, caused much amusement. In the end he had to step among the girls, with his arm cheekily around the shoulders of his photo-pupil, while a friend photographed the group this time. Finally, it transpired that the young amateur photo-grapher was being seen off at the station by her friends, boarding a train in the direction from which he had just ar-rived. So he told her a little white lie, that he was going to the same destination as she and got into the same

compartment. There was a photographic as well as a romantic happy ending to this little story.

I told you this photo-romance not only because it really did happen, but also because it contains a number of practical phototips. Partic-ularly important among them is the example of the light measurement of the back-lighted group. This represented only a part of the much brighter general measuring field of the exposure meter, held at a distance about 17 feet. It is also arguable whether the young lady, who, incidentally, used a color film, did not in any case attempt too much by placing her friends in direct *contre-jour* light in view of the dazzling snow. Be that as it may, it was essential to approach the group with the exposure meter from the camera viewpoint closely enough for the measuring angle to encompass only the group or part of it, entirely unaffected by the lighter and unimportant surroundings. The objection that with this kind of measurement the mountains in the background will be completely overexposed is correct, but can be met with the contention that the desirable correct reproduction of the group is more important.

What is reflected light measurement?

Perhaps you have already heard that an exposure meter is used according to the reflected light method if it is pointed from the camera position in the direction of the subject. The fact that the measuring angle of the instrument roughly corresponds to the angle of view of a normal camera lens easily leads to the assumption that it is always correct to take the reading from the position of the camera. This is quite true for evenly-illuminated subjects with little color- and brightness-contrast. Hardly any differences in the reading would be noticed on approaching the subject more closely. All the same, it will always be worthwhile to base the determination of the exposure time on a close-up reading whenever pictorially important details in a landscape are situated in the foreground, and of which the best possible color reproduction is felt to be an essential feature.

You should also take care that your own shadow is not cast on to the subject while approaching it.

The other trick can be recommended with open landscape subjects which, in spite of full frontal sunlight, show differences between foreground and background. A green meadow reflects less light than the sky. In order to obtain the right "mean", or average, reading, you should tilt your exposure meter slightly downwards – not too much – rather than upwards; if the measurement of the foreground is largely different from that of the sky, the mean between the two results can be chosen as a compromise. All the differences are taken care of with the incident light method, – which will be our next subject.

The incident light method

To say that in this method we turn round through 180° in order to measure in the opposite direction would not be telling the whole story. Strictly speaking, the light measurement consists of an examination of the entire quantity of light incident upon the subject.

We, therefore, generally walk up directly to the subject, taking our measurement in the direction of the camera instead of from the exposure direction, that is from the camera to the subject. But wait a minute – it is a basic feature of the exposure meter that its measuring angle is deliberately restricted; it approximately corresponds to the angle of view of a standard lens.

If we measured the light incident upon the subject from all sides only under this limited angle, we would only utilize a small part, and the reading would be wrong. Therefore instruments permitting incident light measurement are fitted with a special device. In some cases it consists of a roller "blind" which is pushed in front of the honeycomb window.

Other exposure meters employ diffusing plates to be fixed over the measuring window (so long as they have not been lost!). Their effect is to widen the original narrow measuring angle by many degrees. Thus all the light which adds up to the illumination of the subject is utilized to affect the measurement. The young man of our photo love story could, of course, also have measured the light from the group in the direction of the camera. Most likely he would have obtained much the same result as he achieved in the end by approaching the girls as closely as he did. Only, you must not forget during this type of measurement to use your roller "blind" or diffusing plate. This incident light method, as it is called by the experts, is particularly popular in the United States.

With all back-lighted subjects I would use the incident light method first and foremost. No matter how pretty the fringes of light painted by the sun in backlighting – the deep shadows no longer receive much attention. But we are interested in the remaining indirect light! This is merely by the way.

It may also happen that we take an incident light reading with the sun shining directly on our closed roller blind or diffusion plate. In such a case we must shade it without fail, a necessity which is far too little known. We screen it against the sun with the hand at a distance of about 15–20 inches in order to prevent the direct sunshine entering the larger measuring angle.

It will happen very often in practice that with the best will in the world we cannot approach our subject directly in order to take the measurement in the direction of the camera. The advice I am giving you now is also of a more symbolical nature, in order to make the differences between reflected and incident light measurement even more clearly apparent. Should you, for instance, find yourself barred by a small, but marshy stream, winding its course below a dappled sky in *contre-jour* light, you need, of course, not get your feet wet in order to take your incident light measurement according to the Book of Rules. Instead, you point your meter at the sky, to which your back was turned only a moment ago.

In my experience the method of incident light measurement, no matter how plausible it may be in some cases, is less frequently called for than the reflected light method. To make quite sure one can, in the beginning, take readings according to both methods. Provided the instrument is held and used correctly, the results will be identical in the vast majority of cases. This cross-check of the exposure time inspires particular confidence in the meter reading.

If, however, in spite of strict observance of all the rules differences do occur between the two types of measurement sometimes to the extent of a whole stop value, this will be, at any rate, a sign that we shall run the least risk if we use a setting half-way between the two results. I always like to compromise in such cases.

I have dealt with these measuring methods in such great detail not without misgivings. Perhaps you found these pages a little heavy going. Certainly I would like to save you all the theoretical ballast, but the correct use of your exposure meter prevents the failure of pictures which may perhaps be unrepeatable. Moreover, it indeed helps to save you money, and it is no exaggeration to say that even an expensive instrument will rapidly pay its own way with color film. My explanatory notes with the pictures often deal with the technique of measuring, so that I need not go into the matter any further at this point.

Practice versus theory

Already a vast special literature for amateurs has sprung up which tries, in voluminous and sometimes also cryptic discourses, to explain the alpha and omega of color photography. The existence of such books, attempting to interpret the nature of the colors by means of very lucid drawings up to the level of spectral analysis, enables me to leave the answers to the many "whys" to the more theoretical text-books, and to concentrate on practical tips in my own book.

I also avoid all philosophising in connection with color. Many years ago, I read somewhere, and it made me shudder, "that everything we see is an illusion since it depends on light rays, and that the whole world, strictly speaking, is nothing but a great illusion". Frankly, I cannot imagine that even the most profound insight into all the questions of Life and into the problem of the existence of matter could be of any possible use for your harmless, light-hearted weekend trip or your next summer holiday.

I would welcome some of these text-books even more if their authors rested content to explain ultimate theoretical principles clearly without drawing practical conclusions therefrom, which merely mislead the credulous reader. I thus read recently, much to my surprise, that the results of the photo-electric exposure meter would have to be modified by extension factors "where medium and dark colors are involved". This, I am afraid, slide-rule-inspired knowledge leads to the final conclusion that a subject with dark colors in *contre-jour* lighting which was measured at f/5.6 and $1/50$ second would be correctly exposed at four times this value i.e. f/5.6 and $1/12$ (or $1/10$) second. This may be quite right, but then the measurement must have been wrong!

The Dreaded "Color Cast"

Hardly a conversation on color photography passes in which lively complaints are not thrown into the discussion about "juicy color cast". I am now addressing the beginner who is not yet stricken with grief, as well as those who have already suffered from recurring color cast.

Before we go any further, we must distinguish between two basically different disturbances through such color casts. Their causes, too, are entirely different.

For some color casts we can blame neither ourselves nor our exposures. They are either due to the emulsion or the development. Color reversal film in the past has been prone to this fault; it would be foolish to deny this.

The other disturbance, which is not caused by faulty manufacture or development, is basically no color-cast at all, but caused by reflections from neighbouring colored objects which light the subject with their own color.

Having first of all classified my casts in these various groups, let me begin with the ordinary color cast which is – apparently as well as ostensibly – not our fault.

If the entire film from beginning to end shows a color cast which not only deprives the transparencies of clarity and luminosity, but also daubs, as it were, all the lighter color tones with, for instance, a reddish or greenish cast, we must – unfortunately – seek the origin in the material itself rather than in our exposures.

I have already indicated at the beginning of this book what a miracle of chemical and technical work is involved in the color film with its three inconceivably thin layers. The emulsion is checked by continuous controls throughout the whole manufacturing process in order to produce material which is flawless in every respect.

As soon as the film leaves the factory, where during its manufacture and storage it has been protected against all temperature-changes and other effects it may sometimes – perhaps long before it is used – be exposed to bad influences. I do not wish to blame the storage conditions at the wholesalers nor your photo dealers; however, it is a fact that color films should be stored at constant and low temperatures of ideally 65–68 ° F. maximum and at approximately 50–60% atmospheric humidity. Apart from this, never use old, out-dated, color film, whose expiration date has passed.

Let us then assume we start our holidays with a few cassettes of freshly-bought color film. On our return, we find that all the pictures have a color cast.

It is sometimes extremely difficult to trace the cause responsible for this. Mostly wrath is first directed at the developing station, at times the manufacturers accept the complaint and try to make up a little for the damage done, although sending a replacement film does not restore the holiday pictures.

Humidity and temperature changes

To illustrate the subject "holidays and color cast" I must tell you about a case of my own experience, in which I was myself responsible for the trouble. During a September journey to Spain, I had my film store, two boxes containing 10 Agfacolor cartridges each, in the luggage compartment of my car. I did not always want to open my fully-packed suitcases in order to dig for my films. Easy access in the luggage compartment whenever I needed a film appeared to be of particular importance.

Unfortunately, the weather on this journey was, against all expectations, anything but reliable. During the first week high summer temperatures made me curse my Sedan more than once. Occasional parking on shadowless squares made me feel as in an enforced Turkish bath. With windows turned down as far as they would go, and increased speed I tried to cool the overheated interior. The temperature inside the luggage compartment I dared not guess. It must have been akin to that of a hay box, in which our grandmothers used to keep their meals warm.

During the following weeks we had days with breaks in the weather and temperatures which even the village elders could not remember. I still recall with shivers the damp beds in unheated hotels, the damp clothes – in a word – horrible!

However, generally Spain was photographically of such ravishing beauty that during the last week I sent a wire home for five more films. All the films, including the last five, came from the same emulsion batch, that is they bore the same emulsion number. One could not call the results exactly dreadful, but they were disappointing all the same. The films stored in the car showed without exception a green cast which, though it was still tolerable, was noticeable to critical eyes.

On the other hand, the last five, which had been stored at home at even temperatures in a dry cupboard, were perfect!

The useful crop of my Spanish journey thus consisted practically only of the films forwarded to me. Only the comparison between the over-cooked and the forwarded films prevented me from writing rude letters to the developing station or from telling the manufacturers what I thought of their film.

It is therefore important to follow the storage instructions strictly, at home as well as on journeys.

The eye can be deceived

The human eye is a great miracle, but we must admit that its memory for colors is a little shaky. It can therefore be easily deceived.

Why do we take a sample of material, in order to match it with the sewing cotton, out into the daylight to compare it in order to avoid the wrong impression in the "mixed light" inside the shop?

Or another example – a house has a snow-white finish, yet during the course of a sunny day it shows a wide range of color tones beginning with yellowish-red, moving to blue, and returning to yellow according to the height of the sun's position. If we asked anyone, morning, noon, or evening, what color our house was, he would be certain to reply – somewhat astonished and with a questioning note in his voice "why, white of course"!

The human eye, then, sees changes in the illumination much less objectively and correctly than they are registered by the film. Even considerable modifications in the color are automatically allowed for; the expert says, "the eye adapts itself".

You can see this adaptation of the eye particularly well during, for example, the projection of 12 color transparencies in succession, all with a heavy blue cast. After a time, as picture fol-

lows picture on the screen, this cast is no longer found disturbing unless it is altogether excessive. The eye has become accustomed to it! But if in the middle of all these "blue" pictures there appears, accompanied by admiring "ahs" and "ohs" from the viewers, a sunset, its effects will be particularly warm and glowing. And if the blue series is now directly resumed, the eye immediately signals "goodness gracious, how blue!" It is therefore an important point to show the slides during a lecture in the correct order to avoid such shocks. At any rate, it is clear that our eye, far from seeing objectively, sees very subjectively.

The color reflection

On the fresh grass the family, dressed in light summer frocks, are having a picnic, half in the shadow of a little birch grove. The longed-for sun-tan, as outward evidence of a holiday well-spent, has not yet been acquired. The picture is so pretty that you simply have to take a color photograph, but it will most likely have a green cast. Basically, this effect has nothing at all to do with a cast as such. It is the quite natural reflection from leaves and grass which impart their color to objects and people in the shade. The so-called "local" colors of the skin and the light frocks are modified by these reflections. The eye, untrained in the perception of such color phenomena, does not notice

63

this change during the exposure, so that later on it is certain to protest against what it calls this "green cast"!

A similar surprise was experienced by an amateur, proud owner of a snow-white poodle. He had photographed the animal on his terrace, and was disturbed by a slight, buth nevertheless annoying green cast. The explanation was quickly found; on the low parapet of his terrace stood long rows of green flower boxes which had thrown their reflection on to the dog's coat from all directions.

He was then advised simply to include the cause of these reflections in the picture. He took some more photographs and confirmed, highly gratified, that his poodle's coat was white again! But he did not like the picture, because the flower boxes disturbed him. So he masked them on the transparency; on projection, the coat appeared green again!

A beach beauty sitting on a red bath towel will show in her so-called bogus shadow (the part of her body not exposed to direct sunlight) a noticeable red cast, obvious even to the untrained eye. The less suntanned she is, the more evident it will be.

People dressed in white will be suffused with a red sheen when passing a brick wall or a red truck, for example. A face bent over a sun-lit piece of material during needlework or embroidery will appear tinted by the color reflection, depending on whether it is red, green, blue, or yellow. For the same reason, the reader of a newspaper will be properly illuminated with white light, although his face ought, by rights, to be in the deep shadow of *contre-jour* light!

All this is neither a mishap nor a color cast, but a reflection which, by recognizing it in time, we have to learn either to suppress or, if possible, to exploit.

The example of the "green" poodle has already taught us that we can largely cancel the impression of the cast by showing the cause of the reflection in the picture. If, therefore, we take a portrait in the shadow of a red sun-shade, we should not forget to include the shade, or at least part of it, in our picture. Thus the source of the red flood of light engulfing the face is at once apparent. This inclusion of the reflecting source need not always be a compromise – in time, a deliberate technique based on it can produce the most striking effects.

If grass and trees cause green reflections in the shadows, or sunshades result in tomato-colored faces, how much more powerful a source must the biggest reflector of them all be, flooding as it does everything with

64

an all-pervading color. The blue sky above us! Therefore, a pure blue sky, particularly during the summer months at noon, far from being the experienced photographer's delight, is a great source of trouble to him.

Color photographs in the shade without any other direct illumination than the blue of the sky are therefore bound to be in great danger of acquiring a blue cast. And since in many cases we do not include the cause of this reflection in our photographs, we do not accept as true the cool blueness on the white wall and the garden furniture or on clothes and faces.

What then can we do against all these "enemies of the natural color picture"? Well, we shall soon discusss the remedies in detail, but before we do this, we must submit to a short theoretical detour.

What is the meaning of "color temperature"?

Unfortunately, (or perhaps luckily!) I can only touch with a few sentences on a problem which is worthy of treatment at great length in a thick volume. The term "color temperature" occurs so frequently that we should at least know what it is all about. For the question of when and why color casts occur is closely connected with the "color temperature".

The many colors of the world we live in have been divided into "degrees". Just as we have agreed that water should freeze at 32° F., we also conceived the notion to establish a scale for sunlight.

When we look at the white sunlight through a prism we can easily see it split up into the colors of the rainbow; this is a well-known phenomenon. Only, the scientist cannot do much with vague descriptions such as blue, green, and red. In order to determine the color of the light simply, the physicists make use of the familiar fact that glowing bodies change their colors with rising temperatures. We know that an incandescent light bulb running on a low voltage emits a reddish-yellow light, which, however, becomes increasingly white as the voltage is increased. The hotter a glowing body becomes, the higher becomes the proportion of blue in its "white" heat – we only need to think of the example of the glowing iron on the anvil: with increasing heat it becomes brighter, that is less red. Physicists are in a position by means of spectrometry to measure the increase in blue. Thus they can determine, not only at the blacksmith's around the corner, but also in

65

distant stars, the temperatures of incandescent bodies with great accuracy.

If you really want to know it in detail: – the color of the light emitted by incandescent bodies depends on their temperature. It was therefore the obvious thing to express the color of the light by a temperature value. We thus speak of the color temperature, with the Kelvin degree as the unit of measurement.

The scale of these Kelvin degrees begins at –273° C. A black object, hollow and cooled to this absolute minimum temperature, would thus be at zero degrees Kelvin in its light-proof interior. Utter, absolute, black pitch-darkness.

The warmer this "absolute black body" becomes, the higher rises the number of Kelvin degrees. Now this black body of the physicists is only a concept, not a thing to be carried about in one's trouser pocket where (the temperature being at about 98° F., i. e. 310° Kelvin) it would not be an ideal black body any more.

But joking apart. We have designed so-called color temperature meters with which we can determine accurately the number of Kelvin degrees at any moment. Sunlight between 9 a. m. and 3 p. m., for instance, is generally about 5.800° Kelvin. Therefore, daylight color film is sensitised for a mean value of about 5.800° Kelvin.

Yellow interiors

You will now also understand why pictures taken at home in the light of chandeliers or standard lamps on color films sensitised for sunlight always look so yellow. For normal incandescent lamps have a color temperature of only about 2.600° Kelvin to 2.800° Kelvin. In order to reproduce the colors in your own home correctly on a daylight-balanced color film, an illumination of a higher color temperature would first have to be provided. And this is one reason for the great popularity of electronic flash units which, with their sunlight characteristics, permit the continued use of daylight color film in the evening at home.

Or, alternatively, we buy the well-known photoflood lamps (the household fuses must be strong enough, or else !!!) which give a color temperature of about 3.400° Kelvin. This is the value for which the artificial light type A color film is sensitised; at present it is only available as a reversal film. However, if you insist on using daylight film even in this light, you will have to use a conversion filter which adapts the film to the lower color temperatures (p. 84).

In order to determine which filter should be used in any given case a color temperature meter is extremely useful. Such an instrument – to-

gether with a set of correction filters in the hands of experts and discriminating amateurs – appears to me to be a fine thing.

In 90% of all cases we will be able to manage with this rule-of-thumb: daylight color films should be used in daylight, with electronic flash, and blue-tinted flashbulbs, while artificial light color films should be used with yellow-tinted flashbulbs, photoflood lamps, and ordinary incandescent lighting.

To conclude our excursion into the theory of color, I would point out that although the scientist, by means of his Kelvin degrees, describes blue as warm, and red as cold, we should, in our amateur language and as our fathers did before us, call the luminous red warm, and the blue sky cool. This is more in keeping with what our commonsense tells us.

The "Warm" Emulsions

We are justified in describing such color film as e. g. Agfacolor and Anscochrome as having a "warm" tendency which in its color rendering adapts itself more to the subjective color perception of the human eye. In other words: In these emulsions this warmer tendency has been

VEGETABLE MARKET AT FREIBURG, SOUTHERN GERMANY

Have you ever strolled through a colorful market, thoroughly enjoying what you saw?

But no matter how tempting it is – to create a picture of this scene of plenty is not easy. You must confine yourself to a small excerpt and look for lighting conditions which make the subjects appear stereoscopic.

This is not a fruit piece, but a picture of a market. Although it shows only a part of it, everything happens in it that is typical of a market scene – the lively gestures of buyers and sellers in front of a background of old houses. For this, the 35 mm. Summaron is the ideal lens. Even at medium stops it produces a great depth of field and in conjunction with the more sensitive color film permits a short exposure time. And you will need it in order to avoid blurred movements.

As so often, the lens is focused on the front third of the picture – in our case on the plums. As in the case of my fruit piece, the high sun is again obliquely in front of me. Thus, every single fruit is fringed with a delicate halo of light.

Such color photographs of market scenes are really within the range of everyone. Even the otherwise drab, matter-of-fact cities have their market days, and the colors of the fruit and vegetables are the same everywhere. Do not forget the Latin motto pars pro toto!

Leica, 35 mm. Summaron, 8, $^1/_{100}$ second, September, 11 a. m., sunlight.

PROFILE OF A BEAUTIFUL GIRL

This picture, too, – like the preceding one – was taken more or less on the spur of the moment.

We conversed in a small group in bright sunshine. When the intense contre-jour light made me squint a little, I noticed the beautifully-lit profile of the young girl delicately standing out against the greenish-brown background.

In order not to lose the impression produced by my squinting, I quickly replaced the normal 50 mm. by the 90 mm. lens, which I focused on the profile. The closeness of the model (about 5 feet) combined with the long focal length made for a rapid falling off of sharpness towards the background, thereby producing a pictorial effect.

Imagine a background which is not so blurred, but reproduced with all its disturbing detail: the beautiful face of the girl would more or less be glued to the "vegetable" background.

Moreover, everything happened so quickly and had to be done without delay, that in all this hustle I forgot the increased film speed. The result is therefore on the verge of over-exposure.

Leica, 90 mm. Elmar, f/5.6, $^1/_{100}$ second, October, sunlight, about 11 a.m.

deliberately encouraged, and the reproduction of blue repressed because otherwise filters would have to be used during a considerable part of the day in order to avoid an excessive blue rendering and thus an unnatural appearance of the results. It is an established fact that color films with a warm tendency can be used even during the hours of noon between 11 a. m. and 1 p. m. almost without compensating filters except for exposures at high altitudes.

Although I appreciate very much the exact determination of the color

temperature and the appropriate choice of certain filters for color photographs, I fear that taking them ceases to be a pleasurable pastime, a hobby, if we pay too much attention to these corrections. This also has the direct result of a considerable slowing down of the exposure as such, since we lose too much time over choosing the correct filter. I am aware that this point of view is arguable in the face of the almost touching humility with which many of my friends in the States carry three, six, or more filters about with them – but hardly enjoy their photography any more.

I would therefore give you merely the basic advice of carrying only a skylight filter in addition to your haze filter; other, stronger pink filters should only be tried if this appears essential.

Beware of color cast! Talking about these "compensated" color emulsions it must be admitted that the clear advantage of the suppressed rendering of blue can turn into a slight disadvantage in the light of the setting sun, when the light itself will become so warm that the inherent tendency of the film is reinforced. Therefore, Agfacolor photography practically comes to an end two hours before sunset, unless we are willing to accept rather yellow pictures and "Red Indian" portraits at late hours.

Naturally, a yellowish-red character is very popular in some photographs, such as pictures of Alpine glow, auroras, or sunsets. However, it is essential that the cause of such colors should be in evidence, even if its only indication were the length of the shadows indicating a late hour of the day.

Conditions are quite similar early in the morning within two hours of sunrise. Nor does this blue suppression of Agfacolor mean that we are protected against any kind of blue reflections in our pictures. Suppression does therefore not mean cancellation, because otherwise we would be very sorry if we had to do without the beautiful, blue-dominated shadows in our snow pictures.

You may have noticed that up till now I have avoided, as far as I could, the ambiguous term of "blue cast". Basically, everything we generally call blue cast is a reflection. However, the terminological confusion is too great for me to attempt a solution single-handed. If, therefore, I gave the next chapter its correct title "the blue reflection", later on a thousand helpless readers would look in vain for remedies for "blue cast". I give in, then, and follow the common usage.

The Blue cast

The most frequent, prominent, and hence unpleasant of all "casts" is the blue cast. It mainly occurs during the summer around midday; particularly whenever pictures are taken in the shade under a cloudless sky when the blue sky is practically the sole light source instead of the sun, which is more or less indirectly involved only.

I am writing this, trying hard to remain as clear and lucid as I can, in a hotel bedroom at Florence; it is the end of March, and compared with our Western climate the temperature is almost summer-like. My room faces a courtyard, full of noisy children. They are playing in the shade. At this time of the year the sun does not yet rise very high in the sky, and in spite of the midday hour does not reach the courtyard. Only for fun and without any photographic intentions I just hold my color temperature meter against the blue sky as the effective light source for the shady yard. The result: 9.000 ° K. A considerable imposition on a film sensitised for about 5.800 ° K. In spite of this difference I would risk the exposure of the shady yard without correction filter if only it were more attractive photographically. The blue cast present would still be quite tolerably compensated by the color film, and the saturated red and brilliant yellow of the blouses and frocks would improve matters further, as in fact even bluish pictures can be improved by such color effects.

If I sat here in July, my instrument pointed at the sky at 12 a.m. would give me a reading of about 18–20.000°, and I should certainly have to give up any attempt at color photography.

But wait a moment – opposite my window rises a high, white wall of a building. Now during March the sun can light only part of it; nevertheless, the reflection is already strong enough to dazzle me. However, I guess that if the sun stood higher the entire wall would be lit up. Most probably a powerful white reflection from direct sunlight would add so much warm light to the blue shadow that a picture of the courtyard would be worth-while.

My apologies for this excursion, but these examples help us to solve, I believe, the following question more easily.

Clouds as reflectors

For instance, it is surprising to observe how much the blue sky reflection is reduced in the shadows when large white cumulus clouds act as reflectors. They have an effect similar to that of the white wall, lowering the high color temperature. Immediately this results in a much more pleasant light in the shadows. (The difference is only noticeable to the trained eye.) Portraits may then succeed at midday, although it is better generally not to attempt them just at the "high blue hour of noon". The same cumulus clouds which are welcomed by every friend of landscape photography will also have the effect of reducing the blue content of sunlit subjects during midday, at the same time softening the often very heavy shadows.

High clouds produce blue cast

There are clouds... and clouds. Some of them are anything but beautiful. They cover the whole sky and only give us a hint of the sun; nevertheless, the light is so bright that it dazzles our eyes, and then, too, the color temperature will be considerably higher than desired. Landscape subjects, particularly, which somehow lack sparkle in the absence of direct sunlight, acquire a light blue cast, which will only be tolerated if strongly dominant warm colors such as red, yellow, orange, and so on, in the near foreground enliven the picture.

Gray sky can be ideal

Quite contrary to the general opinion, however, the low-cloud sky, even with thick gray clouds and a tendency to rain, is an excellent "studio" for close-up color photographs. Apart from landscape subjects, which may easily appear too feeble and melancholy, close-up pictures of all kinds, portraits, groups, and so on, will be reproduced in this light in their natural colors, unaffected by any cast. If we have not forgotten in such cases to make the appropriate exposure time allowances, the pictures really cannot go wrong. Only, in contrast with direct sunlight as light source, the gray curtain of the sky makes all colors appear considerably more subdued. It is thus not only permitted, but outright essential to include strong colors in our pictures. A brilliant red, in fact all warm colors, help to break up the otherwise inevitable monotony of the dull surroundings.

Hazy light

A whole series of other cases must be listed under the heading "beware of blue cast". I am thinking of the May morning, so popular for a Sunday stroll, when under a hazy sun the more or less subdued phantom scenery is bound to give rise to blue haze in the distance. Nevertheless, the foreground offers fascinating possibilities in color brilliance, only with its contrast reduced by the haziness of the sun.

I experienced a typical example of this once on a journey from Florence to Rome. Although there was very poor distant visibility, the sun gained in strength; nevertheless, the landscape was lost in a milky haze which did not reveal any intensely colored details. All of a sudden, there appeared from a field a brilliant red cart, drawn by two huge white oxen. The entire family, wearing colorful head scarves and carrying very gaudy straw baskets, were precariously perched on the rumbling vehicle. It was like a vision of the countryside, lovely in its vagueness. Without this intriguing veil, in the clear "ideal" light of the sun, I would have produced a nice average photograph abounding with a welter of small detail. The fields, turning green, together with the white and pastel-pink houses, and the oxcart under the deep blue sky would have given me a landscape picture of Tuscany like so many others, but ... without "atmosphere".

I can only quote the old saying "one man's meat is another man's poison" (the North-German version, you might like to know, is "one man's owl is another man's nightingale") and advise you that one can no more establish valid rules of what is good or bad for color pictures, and whether they should be taken in sunlight, haze, mist, or rain, than one can decide any other questions of taste. A manycolored garden gnome in front of a late Victorian Stock-broker's Tudor mansion will send shudders down my spine. The same gnome in a vast park landscape may perhaps look quite attractive. It all depends upon the individual circumstances and the purpose.

There is a time for everything

Your picture of the Kleine Scheidegg (Switzerland) with Eiger, Mönch, Jungfrau, and other famous peaks in the background, taken from the Männlichen in the favourable light of the morning sun, may be so successful that some tourist agency may want to buy it. For a good publicity photograph you will perhaps get more money than you will have to pay for ten or twenty color films. You will be praised and your picture found wonderful (so full of detail).

If on another occasion you only take a tall fir tree and a painted crucifix against a background of heavy cloud, the tourist agency will perhaps have nothing to do with it, but in reality the picture could be far more expressive and better, because it has more atmosphere. Who am I to draw up any rules?

To take a portrait of *Mary Jones* I might choose a day with an overcast sky, since its soft light models her face to advantage and suppresses any possible wrinkles; moreover, *Mary Jones* will want her features to appear "quite natural". On the other hand, the fair curls of the youngest demand the most contrasty lighting by lateral or even *contre-jour* light at the risk that the colors of some details will not turn out quite correctly.

Dr. X's chalet, framed by a mountain range in the background and soft, green Alpine meadows has to wait until a favourable opportunity offers clear visibility, cumulus clouds and "white" sunlight in the morning or afternoon. The tranquil mountain lake, reflecting almost every detail of the surrounding scenery on a calm day, will not make me press the shutter on a windy day. However, when an Atlantic gale howls along the promenade, I hurry to the breakwater or the pier without my breakfast in order not to miss the high breakers with my camera.

A short course of weather lore

There is such a thing as "ideal color weather". To be able to foresee it and not let it clash with an appointment with your dentist you must know a little about the weather. Sometimes a glance at the evening sky and the barometer before going to bed will be enough to be reasonably sure whether the following day will bring "color weather" or not.

What, then, IS "ideal color weather"? The physicist, thinking of his daylight color film, would define it reasonably clearly: "the Kelvin value of 5.800° most suitable for color film is reached when about 1/3 of the blue sky is covered with cumulus cloud. Naturally, the sun must not be hidden at the moment of exposure."

A meteorologist, asked for the ideal weather for color photographs of landscapes will say: "quite simple: onset of anti-cyclonic weather, rear of a cold front, about 3/10 clouds (nothing to do with exposure – it is merely the decimal expression of one third of the sky covered with clouds). And the cold front, and its rear? When there are sudden showers, perhaps even accompanied by hail, we can say with confidence: cold front. These "fronts" move through the meteorological landscape at great speed. And behind them follows, not what the soldier would call the base, but simply and straight-forwardly, the rear.

This rear of a cold front, then, produces chilly, cold, or even stormy weather. The air becomes crystal-clear, precisely the thing we need for distant views. On the other hand, the cloud formations change from minute to minute. If with a pair of good boots and a really waterproof macintosh you tramp through the countryside while the last raindrops still fall from the sky, you will have the best chance of taking color photographs of landscapes under ideal conditions. For the blue gaps in the sky, hardly visible at first, will soon become larger, the clouds break up, and suddenly the sun will illuminate the whole scene.

Moreover, the weather conditions in the rear of a cold front often surprise us with a rainbow, which we could call a color photographer's delight.

The fact remains – only very rarely in the summer will the air be as free from dust, impurities and haze as after the passage of a belt of rain. Perhaps we shall have hazy weather again the following morning! Why not . . . exactly like the case I've just described.

Remedies Against Color Cast

When we were talking about the midday blueness in the shade, I mentioned how bright reflections from a white, sun-lit wall can be of help. The rôle of white cumulus clouds, too, as huge reflectors was emphasized. Applied to more con-  fined spaces, this experience means that a large, spread-out tablecloth can work wonders. We have it arranged as a mirror of the sunlight so cleverly that our subject will be lit up very strongly, without, how- ever, the table cloth itself becoming part of the picture.

During work in the film studios such sun re- flectors are used very often. They consist mainly of large sheets of plywood, covered with silver foil, on special holders which can be turned in any desired direction and fixed at an angle. The larger the surface, the stronger, of course, the effect of the reflection; the closer the mirror is held to the subject, the more in- tensely will it be lit up. We can easily perform the little experiment ourselves by, for example, placing a person in such a position that, although the face is in the shadow, a book or a news- paper on the lap is in full sunlight. The closer the brightly-reflecting surface approaches the face, the more intense will its effect be. Generally, a noticeable difference will already be achieved with a newspaper at a distance of about 20 inches.

Necessity, the mother of invention

I learned most about the practice of softening heavy shadows and gained a lot of experience shortly after the end of World War II. At that time, in Germany, everybody scratched for a living as best he could. As I had been bombed out, I lived with my whole family in a small village in the Black Forest, where the poor remnants of a once formidable photographic array of equipment also found refuge. This consisted of a Leica of considerable age – it is still in perfect working order to-day – a developing tank, and a manual-focusing enlarger. (The story of how these "basic means of subsistence" survived the chaos of the first post-war months, carefully soldered into tin boxes, buried in three feet of soil for 4 months, would be too long, nor does it really matter in this context. Moreover, it is my fervent hope that its practical application will be saved us and the following generations.)

During the years of 1945 and 1946 I visited the farms of the Black Forest with my Leica, taking family photographs. Not so much for the family album as for the identity cards necessary at the time, for which a passport photograph was essential. However, in order to be able to travel to the nearest town, where there might be a chance of obtaining such a likeness, you had to have an identity card. Otherwise the journey could become very unpleasant in view of the numerous controls and checks. It was a kind of vicious circle. The farmers, most of whom lived far from anywhere, were visibly pleased that the photographer himself came into their house, and they and the other members of their families dressed up solemnly for every passport photograph. I have taken many a bad picture in my life, but these beat the lot. For I had to work with long out-dated pre-war films and without any aid of photoflood lamps; into the bargain I had to enlarge on to paper of the same vintage with gray fog along the edges.

The lighting difficulties were grave, because it was not always summer, and it often rained. This made me think of how to solve the problem. The first solution was a file cover with a silver paper covering, which in the absence of direct sunlight brought at least a little more brilliance into my dull, gray peasants' faces by reflecting the brighter sky. Later on, I built a reflector of thin plywood, which could be folded up from all four sides, was also covered with silver paper and could easily be strapped to my latest acquisition, a second-hand bicycle. The silver paper came from a few bars of chocolate, received from some French soldiers in barter payment for a few "full length portraits". You see, photographs, too, can serve as a kind of currency.

Sunlight indoors

I also photographed weddings, and when there was sunshine outside, my artistic temperament began to stir. The "sessions" generally took place in the not-very-light peasants' parlours, since in front of the door (what with dung heaps and all that) the background was mostly less decorative, and any wind would have disarrayed the laboriously arranged hair-do's and veils of the rural brides. So I succeeded, with the aid of the eager youngsters, very ingeniously, in smuggling sunlight from the window or even from inside the house into the peasants' front parlour. At least bride and groom could thus be presented in a favourable light. The effects were reminiscent of Rembrandt!

I hope that this story from the first post-war years has explained to you the value of softening the shadows sufficiently. It is beyond question that in colour photography we are even more in need of this trick, because every softening of contrast results in an improvement of the color rendering, especially in the shadows. You will find a telling example of this kind of lighting on p. 66. The explanatory text describes all the details. They were, considering the high August sun alone, in theory really very unfavourable (high sun = harsh picture), but favourable in practice, because the light surface of the pavement served as a reflector.

Harsh light

Even though a high sun at times eliminates the extreme harshness of the illumination by natural reflections, the fact remains that midday light is unfavourable. This is not only due to its relatively high content of blue, but also because of the more or less vertical incidence of the sunlight.

Nobody, not even a raw beginner, would take photographs without having second thoughts in a room in which a dazzlingly bright lamp is suspended from the ceiling as the sole light source; the type of thing reminiscent of a bare country-station waiting-room. Harsh lighting, which produces dark shadows under the eyes even of young people, does not only make us uncomfortable; it is unsuitable for pictorial photography as a whole.

What then can we do against short, harsh shadows and a blue tendency of the colors on a summer noon? Leave them alone, dear friends, and postpone the picture, if possible, until the afternoon! For even the possible remedy of an anti-blue filter would not be able to cure the harshness of the light.

Daylight flash as a way out

I have reserved most of the questions relating to color photography with flash for a special chapter on p. 146, but I would say here and now that flash is the most appropriate means of making us forget the otherwise scarcely avoidable harshness of midday light. However, this combination of daylight and flash is confined to a circle of about 15 feet because beyond this limit the flash will have lost its effect. The closer the subject is situated, the more carefully must we watch the amount of additional light we have to apply.

Flash is, in fact, the best method, in addition to the sometimes cumbersome expedients of reflecting tablecloths, for giving the impression of well-balanced lighting with pleasantly graded colors. This technique serves us extremely well with very contrasty back-lighted subjects, because it gives us satisfactory color rendering in the deep shadow portions.

For use with daylight color film obviously the only flashbulbs which are suitable are those whose color temperature corresponds with the sensitization of the emulsion. You can, of course, try to soften the shadows with ordinary untinted clear flashbulbs. However, you must then accept a certain shift of the shadow colors towards yellow. Blue-tinted flashbulbs and, naturally, electronic flash too, whose light is largely similar to sunlight, are an improvement in this direction. If the proper dose of light is administered – I like to call it a pinch of flash – even the expert will not recognize at first sight that supplementary lighting has been used. The against-the-light impression will be preserved not only in the shadows, but throughout the picture if the

82

precise amount of flashlight has been added. However, flash is frequently mixed with daylight not only in order to reduce the contrast, but also in order to give blue shadows a sunnier appearance. The correct dose of flashlight, and all the worries about blue cast are over. In the chapter about daylight flash I shall give you all the necessary tips. Other color casts, too, whether red or green, which I have already described in detail together with their causes, will be made to disappear by a flash as by magic. And the body colors will be restored to our subjects.

Something about Filters

With color negative film no correction filters are needed. Instead, we leave the compensation of undesirable color tones to the processing laboratory where sets of printing filters permit a continuous modification of the color character according to requirements. This has now reached the stage where we use one and the same color negative film for both daylight and artificial light irrespective of color temperature.

As we know, these possibilities for control do not exist with reversal film. This poses the question how far the color balance should or could be influenced by the use of filters during the exposure. There are a number of finely graduated correction filters on the market, advertised for the general purpose of "improving color photographs".

Apart from the so-called colorless UV-absorbing filter which has special functions, you can buy, for example, a whole set of six filters, of which three have a slight blue, and three a pink to purple tint in slightly different strengths.

These filters, then, are supposed, singly or in various combinations, to bring the light, ranging between 2.000° K and 20.000° K, to a color temperature most suitable for the color film. In other words, whether candlelight, clear flashbulbs or blue reflections from the mid-day sky, the filters will help in every case (at least in theory).

This sounds very convincing, but in practice is only feasible if we are able accurately to determine any given type of illumination.

"Conversion" filters

Let us assume for the sake of argument that we want to take pictures on daylight color reversal film in artificial light. The normal photoflood lamps only give us a color temperature of about 3.400° K. Without a filter, the film would then show a strong yellow cast in all colors. By using a bluish filter of the density B 12 we adapt the color film; in technical language, we use a conversion filter.

In the rare case when we have an artificial light film in our camera with which to take daylight pictures, we must take a reddish filter of the density "R 12" in order to be able to use our artificial light film like a daylight film. It is quite obvious that this method requires almost double the exposure time since light is absorbed whenever we use a filter. Many of my readers will think it far simpler to load the camera with daylight color film for daylight exposures and artificial light film for photoflood pictures. Certainly, this is precisely what I do, and in an earlier book I simply omitted to mention a detailed list of conversion filters. However, this led to various readers writing me letters to the effect that very frequently they had found themselves in the dilemma of entirely different types of illumination and were therefore in great need of more detailed information about these filters.

If you are interested in these sets of filters with which to convert any possible type of light, ask your photo dealer for lists of various filters manufactured.

Color correction filters

Naturally, these filter sets also contain color correction filters. They are not designed to adapt the film to an entirely different type of light, but merely to make a slight modification of the illumination. Theoretically, the weakest pink filter "R 3" would be used for any color temperature in excess of normal (5.800 ° K), or the bluish "B 3" for the setting sun to counteract the slight yellow cast. However, what do we do when we have to reckon with a really disturbing blue cast or a yellow cast? How are we to find out accurately without a color temperature meter?

I know from my own experience that an adaptation to an altered color balance is possible, but not vitally necessary. The occasional advantage bears no relation to the trouble caused by carrying around with us, and constantly varying, filter combinations. In addition – this is perhaps the most important argument – it is not at all a foregone conclusion that the reduction of color atmosphere by means of filters is always justified. I would not attempt, for instance, to influence by filtering the typical color shift caused by a low sun. Also, blue haze in the distance may sometimes be very welcome in many pictures.

Haze and skylight filters

Some amateurs use a so-called haze filter in order to reduce the blue content. Other amateurs again prefer a "skylight filter".

BOY GOATHERD

*In a small, forgotten village on the south coast of Italy, whose name
I do not remember, and which cannot be found on any map, sits Beppo,
the shy little goatherd, in the porch of a country inn.*

*Inside sits his father, sipping his wine during his lunch break. Beppo
has to wait patiently outside, for a long time. He is quite unaware that
I am just about to take his picture. Most likely he has hardly ever seen
a camera in his life before, certainly not a Leica. This is why he looks
at mee completely without posing. No affected smile, nor any outstretched palm. He sits there, quite simply, as perhaps his forefathers
sat tending their goats, the sole possession of the family.*

*He has not the faintest idea how picturesque he looks on the old
rickety chair in front of the white-washed wall.*

Leica, 50 mm. Summicron, f/2.8, ¹/₂₅ second, room without sunlight, but blue reflections from the cloudless sky. May, about 12 a. m.

IN WIESKIRCHE CHURCH, UPPER BAVARIA

Generally it is forbidden to take photographs inside churches, however, special applications to take pictures other than during divine service will, in most cases, be sympathetically considered.

Often this application must be submitted in writing and sufficient reasons given for it.

All this is, of course, impossible during an impromptu visit to a church. Nevertheless, one may not be able to resist the temptation of trying to take interior views without a tripod. After a glance round out of the corner of one's eye, and with a bad conscience, the camera is propped against a wall, and an exposure of several seconds made, depending on the lighting conditions.

A well thought-out and accurate arrangement of the picture area will be out of the question under such conditions. The illegality of the whole business also deprives the photographer of the peace of mind so necessary for the appropriate treatment of the subject. Small wonder, then, that in most such cases failure is the order of the day. The delight at having got a picture after all is often more rewarding than the quality of the photograph.

In very bright churches there is naturally a better chance of making hand-held exposures unnoticed; with the new, faster colour emulsions, hand-held exposures of $1/10$ second do succeed occasionally, provided that you have a steady hand. An enchanting marvel of lighthearted Rococco architecture such as this cannot fail to encourage you to take a picture of your own. Since the church was empty except for a few visitors, I pressed my Leica against one of the pews, pressing the button with bated breath. The use of a wide-angle lens from a raised standpoint would have been ideal here. But that would have meant a ladder or table and a tripod! Because in photographing interiors we must, in the majority of cases, tilt the camera a little in order to include the whole arch of the ceiling. This easily produces converging verticals which we cannot remove from an original colour transparency.

Leica, 50 mm. Summicron, f/2.8, $1/15$ second, September, about 11 a.m.

Let us briefly point out the difference between the two. A haze filter largely corresponds to the UV-absorbing filter, described in the next chapter, and can be used exactly like it without difficulty. A skylight filter, on the other hand, is designed solely for the general reduction of blue.

While the so-called haze filter can be recommended warmly for all color film emulsions, I can advise the use of the skylight filter only with those color film emulsions which have no inherent blue suppression. At any rate, experiments with the skylight filter have shown that it is only in very rare cases suitable. The subtraction of blue from sea-scapes or summer landscapes very often exceeds the desired degree. On the other hand, comparison photographs in the high mountains were quite satisfactory, because there the excess of blue and ultra-violet was very effectively cut down.

If you possess a skylight filter, I should advise you to use it sparingly with Anscochrome or Agfacolor, that is only in extreme cases of blue suppression. If you want to make quite sure, carry out your own tests and compare the results (once "without", once "with").

The colorless UV-absorbing filter

We know from the advertisements of medical lamp manufacturers that ultra-violet light produces the popular sun-tan. It is also known that during a stay in the mountains, even under an overcast sky, we quickly become sun-tanned. For up there the proportion of ultra-violet radiation is far greater than in the plains, where dust and haze form a kind of ultra-violet filter.

Even an ordinary window pane absorbs ultra-violet light, and basically a UV-absorbing filter has much the same effect as a window glass. However, for photographic purposes it must be carefully polished, optically flat, and mounted precisely.

A UV-absorbing filter thus eliminates the invisible ultra-violet rays. At high altitudes UV light may cause a certain amount of unsharpness in the picture, and its blue content, since ultra-violet is invisible, will exceed the expected degree.

We all can easily determine the effect of a UV-absorbing filter by our own exposure tests "with" and "without". My own comparison pictures in the Alps during the winter hardly showed any difference in the reproduction of sky and snow. On the other hand, the shadows were noticeably changed. The very deep, saturated blue had been visibly altered to blue-green!

The reduction of ultra-violet is even stronger in high mountain regions during the summer. Here, the cutting-off of the blue both in the shadows and as a general haze on slopes, meadows, and patches of snow is even more pronounced. I can therefore warmly recommend the constant use of a UV-absorbing filter during the summer in the mountains at altitudes above 6,000 feet. However, only a so-called "colorless" UV-absorbing filter must be used for color photographs on reversal film. The UV filters normally used with black-and-white films are not suitable!

"Cold" and "warm" lenses

The effect, by the way, of these filters varies individually. The reason for this is that some lenses render the colors "colder", others "warmer", because according to the number and type of their components they absorb ultra-violet rays to varying extents. Mostly these differences are apparent only if a camera is used with interchangeable lenses.

Many an amateur has been working for years with his "Elmar", "Tessar", or "Xenar" without the slightest idea that these four-component lenses belong to the "cold" types which respond particularly well to the use of a UV-absorbing filter. Others, for example those owning a Leitz Summicron, have a "warm" lens without being aware of the fact. The high-quality elements pass much less UV light. In spite of this inherently welcome property – in popular language we could almost speak of a built-in UV filter – my pictures were never the worse for being taken through a UV-absorbing filter even with this lens.

You may be interested to know in this connection that all my lenses are permanently fitted with UV-absorbing filters. Not by any means out of fear of Ultra-Violet, the Invisible, but in order to protect, once and for all, their highly valuable and vulnerable front elements from any possible damage. It simply must be accepted that the glass is very easily touched by mistake, and a finger mark is caused. With care it can be removed with a very soft cloth, just as dried-up water marks, and any possible deposits of dust are removed from time to time with soft chamois leather or a sable brush. As long as this is done gently, you need not be afraid of causing any damage.

But I believe that the way I proceed during a quick interchange of lenses is not always correct. In order to waste no time, a lens will occasionally slide into a trouser pocket to join company with a bunch of keys and loose coins; in such a case the UV filter permanently screwed-in is an ideal window, behind which the precious eye of my camera is protected as in a glass case. After all, such a UV filter is much cheaper than the repair and the repolishing of a lens.

You see, I even photograph with a guard against UV when it is not necessary.

A special case: the polarizing filter

My first encounter with a polarizing filter lies far back. It was before my color photographic period when I watched a photographer shooting some interior shots, partly because I was interested, partly in order to be allowed to carry cameras and tripods. Instead of the yellow, green, orange, and red filters with which I was already rather familiar at the time, he used for these pictures a polarizing filter.

Now this filter, which appears dark gray when it is held against the light, has nothing at all do with snow- and ice-pictures in polar regions; it has other mysterious properties. With it my professional photographer could make disappear as by magic, or at least reduce, reflections and highlights. I learned from his practice that disturbing reflections are eliminated by this filter, and that a still life, or whatever it is, can be photographed almost without any reflection.

The whole secret of the polarizing filter which I call polar filter for short, rests on the fact that reflected light is partly polarized on non-metallic surfaces such as glass, water, wood, plants, oil paints, etc., when it behaves differently from non-polarized light in its plane of vibration. A filter incorporating a special "screen foil", the polar filter, has the property of extinguishing the polarized light vibrating from the reflecting surface, while it transmits the non-polarized light without difficulty.

Most probably we need a detailed explanation in order to understand this phenomenon. However, my passing mention of the properties of polarization is merely meant to jog the memory of all those who paid attention during physics' lessons instead of shooting paper missiles at their classmates with rubber bands.

Luckily even those who happened to be away from school at the time will be able to recognize the action of the polar filter plainly without knowing anything about the physical process involved. All you have to do is to ask your photo dealer to demonstrate one to you in front of his shop entrance. The reflections which are always present in the shop windows – which make us walk up to them more closely during daytime in order to see the display without disturbing reflections – are extinguished if you look through the polar filter. Rotate it slowly round its axis, as you would a genuine cut diamond you wanted to examine for its "fire".

If in addition the sun is out and part of the sky clear, you should hold the filter at right angles to the sun, against the sky. After rotating it slightly, you can clearly observe the polarizing effect; at a certain point of rotation the sky will suddenly appear considerably darker because part of the sky light is polarized and filtered out. A consequence with an interesting bearing on our color photography is that clouds, for example, will stand out against the darker sky much more noticeably without any falsification of the color values of the other portions of the subject. However, the degree of filter action varies with the extent of extinction – part or complete – of the polarized light by rotating the filter. Also, on this factor depends the astonishingly large filter factor which at complete polarization should be calculated at $2^{1}/_{2}$ to 3 times.

The dramatized sky

From my own practice I can only say that although the possession of a polar filter is not an essential item of an amateur's outfit, it enables him to take pictures whose effect cannot be achieved in a similar way by any other photographic means.

The polar filter in color photography plays a role much like that of the orange or red filters in black-and-white photography. I am sure you have already seen pictures in which dazzlingly white clouds stand out against an almost black sky. Or photographs where a hazy landscape has been "cleared up" by the use of a red filter (this "demisting" is, however, solely achieved at the expense of atmosphere). At any rate, orange- and red-filtered black-and-white photographs often have a striking and fascinating effect, by showing an unusually dramatic expression due to the strongly modified gradation of the grey tones.

"Polar filtered" color photographs give an impression which, if not quite the same, is closely related. In addition to the improved rendering of the clouds, any general blue cast will also be strikingly reduced – its origin, of course, being the blue reflection of the sky from sand, grass, asphalt, and so on.

Moreover, the polar filter also absorbs ultra-violet completely.

Exposure increase with polar filters

This is what happened to me on the proverbially blue Mediterranean which appeared deep green on polar filter photographs, because the body colors of the algae and other marine flora, growing on the bottom of the sea, showed through when the surface reflection was removed. On the same occasion I also discovered, by means of my beloved exposure test series, the antidote, which should be used in order to take the gloom out of the polar filter effect. I found that an even longer, say 4–5 times exposure, with the polar filter destroyed the exaggeratedly inky impression of sky and sea, while at the same time it preserved the polarization effect in a pleasing manner.

Let us therefore confine all this polarizing business to those cases where sufficiently strong light and flat illumination by the seaside or in the mountains enable us to indulge in increasing our exposure time several times without the need of a tripod. And, please, never forget to determine beforehand whether you want the picture to be vertical or horizontal. For if the filter when adjusted for maximum visual effect is transferred to the camera in exactly this position, it must not suddenly be rotated through 90° or tilted in another direction. Otherwise the polarization effect will be completely ruined, and the whole picture will be several times overexposed. I should also like to make a point of mentioning that polar filters should be absolutely colorless. They must show no more than a slight gray tint. This was not always the case with older polar filters – nor was it very important as they were used for black-and-white photography. However, in a color transparency we would, in addition to the desired dramatization, have to accept a general yellow-green muddiness. Finally, to the color negative fans I would say that they, too, can make use of the polar filter. For although the magicians in the color laboratory can do much, they cannot dramatize the sky without leaving other parts of the picture unaffected.

A few hints about subsequent color corrections

I would not like to conclude the chapter about filter questions without mentioning that we shall soon have an easy and reliable method of improving transparencies, whose colors are not quite up to expectations, at a later stage.

We do not want to go into the question here whether we are faced with a color cast or a color reflection, whether the color balance has been upset by the lighting, the film, the color temperature, or even by the development. All we are faced with is simply an unpleasant cast in some of our transparencies, and we are looking for a possibility of changing or eliminating it. Messrs. A. Faber, photo-chemical manufacturers of Neu-Isenburg near Frankfurt-on-Main, have produced various chemical substances with which color casts in color transparencies can later be removed by dyeing. The idea as such is not new, and baths have long been known for this purpose. At any rate, Faber's did improve considerably a number of faulty transparencies from my collection, which I sent to them as "guinea pigs".

The additional dyeing with one or two colors intensifies the natural color composition of the transparencies. This means in fact the salvage of slightly overexposed transparencies with color casts, which would otherwise clash with the rest of a series. However, I do not wish to be rash. It is Faber's principle not to sell solutions whose first use is also their last. Your photo dealer will tell you as soon as their products are perfected sufficiently for general release, and when they are available.

Naturally, transparencies can also be improved by dry methods. Extremely thin gelatin color filters, in complementary colors, when bound up with the transparency, correct slight color casts in a completely satisfactory manner. You cannot imagine how precious these foils are from their mere appearance. Foolishly I once ordered a large supply from Messrs. Lifa, to be prepared for all eventualities. I found out that a single 2 × 2" foil cost me about 15 cents (this adds up, you know!).

A few words about the lens hood

The lens hood is also called a sunshade. However, neither name is comprehensive enough to describe the universal usefulness of this little piece of metal. We all know that the lens hood is used in order to protect the lens against stray light rays not emanating from the subject; otherwise light directly entering the lens might spoil the picture. This naturally applies also to artificial light and flash exposures. Yet another incidental function of the lens hood is the elimination of side light, which mischievously tries to enter your lens even from outside the field of view of the camera. It is not necessary to establish this fact physically, as it is a frequently experienced and often lamented occurence.

Even pictures made in full front light without lens hood could yield weak results with distorted colors. This happens especially easily in snow and beach scenes, because "stray light" (I know no better description) plays havoc here. Thus, in the absence of a lens hood, we will not only obtain flat pictures, but also lack of sharpness caused by "illegitimate" refraction of rays inside the lens which are not involved in the formation of the image.

Moreover, the lens hood guards against raindrops, splashes of water, snowflakes, etc., and also reduces a little the unavoidable deposition of dust on the front elements of the lens.

Admittedly, the lens hood is yet another gadget to be tucked away here or there in the heat of battle if it is no longer needed. I am no better than my small son, whose pockets, every night, disgorge pieces of string, pocket knife, pencil, and pennies, except that with me the list of contents includes a lens hood. Where on earth, can one put it, if the ever-ready case does not close as soon as the thing is stuck on the lens?

Leitz have devoted a lot of thought to the problem, to which they have recently found a really ideal solution. The lens hood is fitted with spring-loaded tongues which after light finger pressure engage in the front rim of the lens so firmly that the whole Leica could be picked up by the lens hood if you were so inclined. After use the useful little gadget is simply turned round and pushed over the lens like a slouch hat. Thus, we are at long last able to accommodate our universal and essential metal tube in an ever-ready case.

Naturally you need not stop taking pictures because you have forgotten your lens hood, although I have prophesied flat and unsharp horrors. A house doorway, the shadow of a tree, an umbrella, and, in an emergency, even a hat or the hand of your companion held above the lens can take the place of the lens hood – but all these remain only makeshift measures. And you must take good care that the makeshift measure does not appear in the picture!

Memories of Dr. Paul Wolff

Hitherto I have tried to create the technical basis for your own practical color photography. I have chosen this sequence with some forethought. For what use to you would all the advice for better (better in the sense of "original viewpoint") pictures be in the following chapters, if you were not sufficiently familiar with terms such as color cast, reflected light, exposure measurement, and contrasty lighting?

When I began to take photographs almost 30 years ago, I wanted to reach the top quickly – in double-quick time! I admired the "big shots", was fascinated by the pictures of Paul Wolff, made the round of all photographic exhibitions within reach, swetted through books and, of course, had a strong urge to become just as good in the shortest possible time. I watched and was amazed, as one is amazed about a balance act in a circus, with whose seemingly playful weightlessness we forget too easily the amount of work, training, and knowledge involved in its complete mastery.

Thus my first pictures were bound to be disappointments. The first ones? For years and years I pushed the button in my own sweet way and was, indeed, for a long time convinced that lack of basic knowledge could be made up for by a more expensive camera. I thought it would be enough to give my pictures a personal note by simply taking them lying down on the ground instead of from the usual eye-level. I used a red filter, because I had seen impressive photographs in which white clouds towered into a pitch-black sky. The attempt to save the completely underexposed negatives foundered in the incorrectly made-up intensifier. I visited places where someone else had made good pictures and in despair looked for the viewpoint of my successful predecessor, without a clue that the position of the sun and the season were against me. I considered the lens hood a troublesome precaution and proudly dispensed with the tripod at one tenth of a second, because I had hit several bull's eyes at a shooting competition. In short, my memories of that period show with painful clarity a very precocious and rash novice of photography. That I was on the wrong track I learned from Paul Wolff.

When once I showed him my pictures, he patiently explained to me all my mistakes without, however, discouraging me.

Abroad with Paul Wolff

On another occasion, on a cruise together, I served him as a caddy, as it were, like a little boy carrying golf bags with different clubs after his master. Of course, I was pleased to be able to do this, because during the daily contact with his work I could learn a lot.

On this trip Wolff had a clearly defined task. He took black-and-white and color photographs of the life on board and during shore trips from our ports of call. We took the little Chinese boys in the ship's laundry by flash, immortalized beef carcasses on film, shivering in the deep-freeze compartment, and, pestered by flies, picked our way warily through Eastern bazaars, grateful for every spot of cooling shade. We stood by the quayside in the black of night, in order to photograph the white liner framed in light, at six minutes' exposure time; the glowing cigarette was our only light source for setting the stop or looking at our wrist watches. My alarm clock would rudely awaken me from my dreams at 6 a.m., because Wolff wanted to be the first ashore, as the way to Castello X was far more comfortable with the sun still low.

Of course, everyone on board ship soon knew who the prominent passenger was, and I did my best to polish his halo even brighter, basking (without any right to do so, I am sure) a little in his reflected glory.

During our work we were constantly surrounded by a crowd of enthusiastic holiday-makers with cameras. But, of course, it was the more active amateur photographers on board who were particularly interested. They were fascinated by our activities, and more than once I was pumped for detailed information about stops and exposure times. Naturally, they also nibbled at our subjects.

However, everything depends on the man behind the camera. The following example, which occurred again and again, is an amusing illustration of this.

In the "script" of our cruise we had picked a scene which repeated itself every morning as the symbol of relaxation and the comfort of a pleasure cruise. About 11 a.m. a steward appeared on deck in a snow-white uniform serving dainty, appetizing sandwiches on a large tray. He was followed by a colleague with iced fruit juices the mere

sight of which made you gulp thirstily in anticipation. The passengers, however, were lazily reclining in their deck-chairs against the background of the vast, blue sea.

Without much understanding at first I followed Wolff's method of preparing his pictures. At least half a dozen times he would step back, checking everything through the view-finder, judging picture area and color distribution. Here a chair was moved a couple of inches, there a colored sunshade tilted a few degrees, in order to show more of its area and surface. In the background a ship's officer, specially detailed by the Captain as a "model", talked with passengers and had to step back a little in order to reveal the name of the ship painted on a life-belt. Or the steward, with softly tinkling glasses, bent a bit lower still to a deck-chair, because otherwise some feature in the background would appear to grow out of his head. Also, the hand of the model being served with sandwiches and slowly warming fruit juices was raised in an expectant gesture. Even the position of the plate was changed: "a bit further over, just a little more, hold it now!"

I suffered in silence and watched apprehensively a cloud which threatened to darken the sun just at the vital moment. But nothing would disturb Wolff. When he had finished his pictures and thanked his subjects for their general co-operation with a few friendly words, the others, the photo-poachers, had long walked away with several photographs in their cameras.

On board there was not only a staff photographer, but also an assistant who had to develop and print the amateurs' snaps. Often at night I sat with him in familiar surroundings, wreathed in the well-known darkroom smells which, worse luck, during rough weather drove me to the railing more than once. Nothing encourages seasickness quite as much as a rolling, badly ventilated darkroom!

Well, this was my opportunity of having a look at the photographs of the others. Here it dawned on me why Wolff carried out his work with such meticulous thought. His pictures, which later appeared as the best advertising photographs of the Hamburg-America line, were, from the viewpoint of his, but only his, camera, perfect and balanced to the last detail. But everything that others took to the right or to the left of him or even over his shoulder, although it represented the same scene, often showed disturbing intersections or perspective exaggerations. Naturally, the harmonious distribution of horizon, sky, the sea, and so on, also differed widely.

Here you might object that such scenes, posed with much effort and patience, have little to do with the live snapshots which the amateur loves. But please do not forget that these were commissioned pictures in which in a lively and pleasing form everything was to be seen that the future ship's passenger had a right to expect of a pleasure cruise. (And because it is sometimes so difficult to achieve effective publicity with objective photography, many advertising agencies retreat into commercial art, because this permits beautiful simplifications.)

Not all Paul Wolff's pictures took so long to create. Often he saw the right field of view without looking through the viewfinder. The camera still hidden behind his back, his decision was already made about viewpoint, vertical or horizontal picture. With the utmost concentration he quickly pounced with his Leica. Watching him at work you realized that he had gone through a good (and hard!) school!

Photography unshackled

Wolff, by the way, used to be a medical practitioner in Alsace. Not until after the first World War did he become a photographer, and soon made a good name for himself in Frankfurt-on-Main, his new home, with pictures made with large plate cameras – and great physical efforts – because exposure material and equipment in those days were really heavy. It is one of the strange coincidences that the Grand

101

Old Man of the Leica achieved results with a large camera, which one day earned him a Leica as a competition award. At first (it was in the year 1926) he did not take the "little thing" very seriously, and used the Leica only as a "scrapbook". The idea of expecting his fastidious customers to accept Leica enlargements instead of contact prints from plates did not occur to him. Nor was it, in those days, technically possible with the films available.

Only a few years later did the photographic industry produce fine grain films of considerable sharpness, and the term Leica film, still in use for 35 mm. material to-day, was created.

The technical basis was thus established – and the rapid rise of Paul Wolff began. At long last, the laborious approach of the old-time photographer was a thing of the past, and he was really able to go after his subjects with his camera. The live Wolff photos introduced a new style.

It is Dr. Paul Wolff's great merit to have discovered "photography without shackles" and to have spread it far and wide. Heavy cases of equipment and sparing use of material gave way to the miniature camera in the trouser pocket and the successful attempt to approach difficult subjects gradually by means of exposure series. And the best picture from such a series was the fascinating, exuberant Wolff photo. A technique which even today has not yet seen any basic improvements.

From Button Pushing to Photography

It is a moot question whether photography is or is not an art. Nor can the taking of photographs be narrowly defined as a handicraft or a playful spare time occupation.

Photography, my friends, can be more than a pastime or a handicraft. However, the first stage is indeed mostly pastime; the capturing of pleasant impressions, the recording of pleasant memories. The word "snapshooting" expresses this very appropriately. However, this is by no means meant in a derisive sense. After all, haven't we all passed through this stage, or, perhaps, are still in the middle of it? The first school outing with group pictures, confirmation, an afternoon in the café garden with our once adored first love by our side (oh what funny hats!). Then the wedding, the christening, summer holidays at the seaside, then again groups, groups, followed by yet more groups. Here and there single pictures and even portraits, which, however, unfortunately hover a little lost above the bottom edge of a horizontal print.

And among all these many photographs there are only very few which attract the attention not only of the author or those who "had the picture taken", but also of others; here the picture of a foggy autumn morning; there a sunset with reflections dancing across the water; or winter's first snow with a few footsteps losing themselves in a lonely background.

With such pictures, which are not run-of-the-mill, we have captured something. Perhaps it is due to the atmosphere of the photograph affecting us, maybe it was our mood which expressed itself here? Yes, here we tried – unconsciously perhaps – to make a statement, and we succeeded! These are the first faltering steps to express ourselves with a camera, to make ourselves understood. And here is the dividing line between button-pushing and photography.

Some never reach the other side of this critical boundary. They never progress beyond the snapshot collections of photographic memories, indifferent to every pictorial composition and expression. But photography can be turned into a genuine hobby! Exactly as with growing flowers, the first consideration is the desire to create something original.

BRYCE CANYON, UTAH, U.S.A.

Nobody coming here and looking into the rocky valley below could fail to be gripped by a feeling of loneliness and awestruck by the grandeur of Nature. This is Bryce Canyon in Utah, discovered by white settlers only 100 years ago, when they penetrated the dominion of the Redskins. Rows upon rows of jagged teeth looking like glowing pinpoints; silence, utter stillness all around, reaching to the horizon. For thousands and thousands of years water, wind, and weather have engraved their marks in the red rock. In the glowing reflection of the sun the rocky peaks shone from the brightest copper to the deepest terracotta red in the crevices and gorges of the eerie mountain ranges.

I owe it to the oblique light that a white fringe of light crowns the jagged ridges, foreshortened like stage props. In the background the bare wall of rock rises sombrely to the pale sky, for which I deliberately left little space in the picture, in order to emphasize the size and depth of the canyon.

Leica, 35 mm. Summaron, f/11, ¹/₅₀ second, April, 10 a.m., sun in glancing *contrejour* light.

104

RODEO AT TUCSON, ARIZONA

Not three seconds ago the men in the foreground had flung open Horse Box No. 8, and the animal shot out with a wild leap in the air.

Helpers and press photographers, waiting for the unavoidable moment when the cowboy ist thrown from his saddle, keep at a respectful distance. Nobody knows what the bronco will do next, because it is, of course, one of a half-wild variety not yet broken in to tolerate a rider.

With foresight – or so I thought – I had secured a seat directly above the boxes, for here was the scene of most of the activities. Quite so, but I was too close for the standard focal length lens to cover every essential feature of the spectacle. Thus, the wide-angle lens came into its own here. You can see how the second picture field not only includes the wide open gate and the fight going on behind it, but also affords an oblique glimpse of the narrow box directly below, where another cowboy is just about to try scrambling on to his mount.

Here, too, I had my "favourite lighting" – contre-jour light; with frontal light, the thrown-up dust would not have been so clearly visible, and the atmosphere of excitement would be absent from the picture.

Leica, 35 mm. Summaron, between f/4 and f/5.6, $1/250$ second, sunlight, 11 a.m., March.

However, in order to draw from the abundance of photographic possibilities, we must learn how to see. This is not only a matter of talent, it can really be learnt, if only there is a spark of enthusiasm and the wish to make better pictures.

However, in time every hobby demands increasing expert knowledge if it is not to become monotonous. In order to become a painter you need more than a velvet beret and long hair; a chromium-flashing camera with umpteen lenses alone does not turn you into a good photographer. And, if possible, your equipment should keep in step with your increasing knowledge. The ambitious photographer should consider this – above all, everything depends upon the man behind the (good) camera. Let him be an amateur by all means. But he must feel his vocation.

Photographic vision

Experience and observation show us that the impression received by the eye is something quite different from the picture recorded by the camera.

Naturally, one of the most important reasons for this difference is that in contrast to the one-eyed camera we see with two eyes, that is stereoscopically.

Apart from this, the camera records the picture rigidly in an oblong or square frame. And this limitation, together with lines, shapes, and colors forms an integrated whole which in turn forms the picture. On the other hand, our eye scans a field of view which is not confined within any frame with fixed limits. It perceives, in rapid sequence, a large number of individual pictures. Through a complicated thought process they are integrated into a general impression.

Perhaps you might like to try your own experiment. You only see sharply whatever you happen to look at at the moment. Due to the speed with which you change distant and near focusing points, you will be hardly aware of this integration. (How quickly we can do this I remember from school. During examinations our master used to stand by the window, apparently looking outside impassively, until suddenly his voice rang out: "Benser, your copy book lies in front of you, not in front of your neighbour!")

If visual impression and camera expression were not something basically different, every picture, correctly exposed, would automatically

108

become a good photograph. All we would have to do would be to take up position where there was an attractive view, press the button and leave the rest to the color film.

Instead, we very often only produce a very disappointing copy of reality ("you cannot imagine how beautiful the peach- and almond blossom were that year" ... "quite possibly, but on your transparencies they looked like trifle!") I am afraid that more than 90% of all who take photographs in color succumb again and again to this deceptive visual impression. My admission that very often I commit the same error even to-day is by no means based on false modesty. It happens particularly when I am in a hurry or not in a photographic mood.

Please understand me correctly. We do not, of course, want to apply strict judgments to every souvenir snapshot. When we record some funny incident during a holiday trip, we need not call at once for creative photography. Likewise, an occasional panoramic view as a souvenir or a memory prop will be quite justified.

I am sure that every button-pusher has the wish to take better photographs. He wants to be able to present his pictures even to critical eyes unconcerned with the emotional aspect of the picture. For we see our own pictures with our emotions, a thing we cannot expect of the un-involved viewer. He sees more with his intellect, besides having more distance!

It is part of taking better photographs to look carefully through the camera viewfinder ten times as often as one takes a picture. View-finder – and ground-glass screen image – do not both isolate a part from the large field of the eye? This cutting-out thus compels the eye to obtain an approximate idea of the future photograph. The more accurately and clearly a viewfinder shows this frame, the easier it can be judged.

Look before you leap ...

Since not everybody is the owner of a Leica whose new bright-line field-of-view frame represents a type of subject viewfinder which would de difficult to beat, we must also look for simpler aids which force the eye into a frame. They are designed to help us arrive at a firm decision as to whether or not our subject is worth pressing the button.

It is generally known that it becomes easier to imagine the subject without disturbing surroundings, or even to eliminate them altogether, if an oblong formed by thumbs and index fingers of both hands is held in front of the eye. With some practice and imagination this expedient is of some value. Even better is a piece of black cardboard with a postcard-size window cut out of the centre. One eye is closed to exclude stereoscopic vision and the future picture assessed within its margins.

I must confess that I have often recommended this somewhat antiquated trick without having tried it myself until quite recently. The thought of wandering about with a sizeable piece of cardboard in my hand while everybody turned round with amusement did not appeal to me greatly.

In the end I made this "idiot's subject viewfinder" after all and realized with shame and wonder that the cardboard frame is nothing less than a marvellous gadget for compelling the eye to critical judgment before the exposure.

Naturally I do not expect you to enlarge your photographic equipment by half a square yard of cardboard. The use of my own is confined to my own back garden. But do try it out if you want to demonstrate particularly strikingly either to yourself or to others the difference between visual impression and camera view. (By the way, the postcard-size window will indicate with great accuracy the field of view of a standard lens if you hold it from the tip of your nose at the distance of the outstretched fingers of your hand – cocking a snook, schoolboy fashion.)

Whether we use cardboard frame or optical subject viewfinder, they alone do not protect us from disappointments, unless we acquire some more experience in color photography.

There are still quite a few hurdles to be overcome!

We do not, with standard cameras, take photographs stereoscopically and according to our visual perception – our eyes are capable of looking "around" objects. This deprives the pictures of something which I can only describe as "airiness". "Airiness" should by no means be confused with the lack of the third dimension, because even well-taken stereo pictures are still without this quality of airiness.

Furthermore, neither the color transparency nor the color print on paper are capable of reproducing light contrasts as vigorous as the eye can see them in actual fact. Nor can even the best color film under the best possible exposure and processing conditions equal Nature completely in its color reproduction.

All we can do is to make the best of it. Only very critical assessment of the potentially photogenic subject, forethought supported by previous experience, observation of the light and its color composition and finally the choice of the correct viewpoint, are, roughly speaking, the most important signposts on the way of the photographically conceived picture.

All this sounds a little like the opening speech of a headmaster to his new First-formers. On reading it through I relive even now my feelings of apprehension. But perhaps it will reassure you a little to know that with every color film I receive back from the developing station I always make a resolution, in the face of my mistakes, to do better next time.

But let us return to the subject. It has often occurred to me that the picture field appears more colorful to the eye through a window from which I have stepped back a little. If I approach the window more closely, with the frame, as it were, receding, the picture often tends to become paler.

If, for instance, you travel through the countryside by car, looking to the left and right of the road for subjects, you will perceive the rapidly passing scene or landscapes differently, more compactly, that is within a frame. Since it would obviously be impossible to make an exposure during the journey, you will stop the car here and there in order to walk back a few yards. Arrived in front of the just-discovered picture, you will be disappointed because it is not as interesting as it had promised to be after all.

Why is this?

Because the frame is lacking, and the surroundings interfere. Do not despair in such a case, take a little time, and look, at your leisure, for some demarcation. Often a branch is sufficient to frame a landscape and to give you back your lost subject.

An ideal optical subject viewfinder

If you have ever looked through a viewfinder of a Leica M 2 or M 3 you know what is meant by a "brightline measuring viewfinder".

In this viewfinder the field of view of the lens is seen within a silver-bright rectangular frame, which is always needle-sharp and clear, whether you look at a mountain range in the background or the tip of the nose in a face three feet away. However, this is not everything you see. The surroundings of the field of view, too, remain under accurate control. By a slight change in our camera position we can now include this, that, or the other surrounding feature in our picture.

Since the rangefinder image is visible within the viewfinder field at the same time, this permits us to be ready for action with continuous observation of the ideal picture frame. This almost unbeatable combination of picture control and speed of operation has gained so much ground that among experts the superior action-readiness of the viewfinder camera as compared with the reflex camera is never called in question. Since with the introduction of automatic parallax compensation for close-up subjects the well-known and dreaded cutting off of important features of the picture (heads, hats, ears, etc.) is avoided, the advantages even of the single-lens reflex camera have lost their point. However, this does not mean that the reflex principle does not offer many a convenience during the use of longer focal lengths, a fact with which I am going to deal later.

You determine the picture area

If you have ever taken black-and-white pictures you will know the strong effect of a cleverly chosen picture area. An enlargement can separate essential features from unessential ones and achieve afterwards what we failed to achieve during the exposure.

This is the main reason why enlarging in one's own darkroom is such a source of pleasure. The pleasure behind the camera is continued in front of the enlarger. You can cut off boring, empty foregrounds and omit disturbing details at the picture margins. A small change in the format, a tiny increase in the ratio of enlargement, and the snapshot becomes a photograph.

The situation is different with color reversal film. Here we must decide the picture area before we make the exposure. The color transparency with a yawning, empty foreground or an excessively high, overpowering, pale sky, at times demands radical masking before projection, no matter how perfectly it was lit and exposed.

It is completely obvious that the closer we are to the subject, the larger does it appear not only to the eye, but also to the camera. However, what looks to our eyes still reasonably clear in the middle ground of the picture will be reproduced at a diminished size with a camera with a standard lens.

Fill your frame

I do not know what prevents so many amateurs from showing what they want to photograph really large.

Just watch your fellow hikers at a beauty spot. See how they mutually "take" each other: in front of a statue, for instance, for all the world like the Field Marshal up there on his prancing steed in expression and posture. Maybe they really wanted to take home the proof, black-

113

and-white or even in color, of having been there; photographic evidence, as it were. But if you do want evidence, at least it should be clearly recognizable.

Instead, Mr. and Mrs. Button-pusher retreat about 30 to 40 feet with the laudable intention of not cutting off the statue's head and start shooting. If these good people only knew how much clearer the faces

of their fiancées, aunts, and uncles would turn out if they arranged them at a maximum distance of 12 feet from the camera! They would then achieve their ambition: the picture of the sightseeing attraction *and* Aunt Elizabeth's friendly smile!

Please do not take this as a personal attack! Even more I wonder why the larger percentage of all amateur pictures is taken in the horizontal position, when it really ought to be obvious that these very subjects cry out for a vertical frame. But no, our friends walk back, further and further, until at last everything is "in it", wasting space to the left and wasting space to the right which really had no business to be in the picture at all.

It is an old experience, and often mentioned, that in color photography, too, the pictorially essential features should, if possible, fill the frame, or at least dominate it. This should not be taken quite literally; it will be perfectly satisfactory if the surroundings are hinted at. Dont't we often want to know where we had been at the time, whether Alpine meadow, beach, or our own garden? If it is our object to take a full-length picture of a person, we should make sure that he – or she – takes up about two thirds of the picture height (vertical position!). At a camera distance of 9 feet it will be just about right.

Have you ever taken color photographs of a carnival procession? Or a village fête? In most cases this is done from ground level, although the better – and photographically more favourable – viewpoint is obtained from a raised position. And haven't you also had the experience that such a view of many fancy dresses and folk costumes is frankly a little disappointing in most cases? If once again you take a close-up picture of a particularly attractive figure, perhaps only head and shoulders, you will prefer this photograph, if you look at it critically, to those showing mass scenes.

Naturally, there are also very impressive views of whole fancy dress groups and processions. However, their special appeal invariably consists either of their having been taken against the sky as the dominant background, or from an elevated camera standpoint. For this gives us a certain compactness of forms and colors.

Quiet areas of color instead of small color spots

Here we have one of the most important secrets of successful color photography. Far too few of us know that large quiet areas of color have a far more convincing effect than many small color dots and splashes distributed at random all over the picture.

A good example of the validity of this experience may be a visit to Holland during the famous tulip blossom time. This very beautiful display of flower growing raised to a fine art, annually attracts more than a million sightseers. At Easter, or even as late as Whitsun, flower lovers meet in a relatively small area, hardly larger than that occupied by a medium-sized large city. On such days the throng of people and cars filling the roads leading through the fields is downright frightening! The seat on the upper deck of a bus is often the only chance to see anything of the gorgeous show of tulips and hyacinths.

Things are much the same in a famous large park called Keukenhof. From April until the end of May this enchanting piece of earth glows with a multitude of horticultural works of art. Thank Heavens, cars are not permitted there. Nevertheless, on sunny holidays the number of admiring, happy sightseers assumes fantastic proportions.

If you are lucky enough still to be able to see the flowers, you will soon enter a state of inebriation (perhaps the intoxicating scent of the hyacinths has something to do with it). One can see amateurs who normally husband their resources of color film very carefully, acting without any restraint at all. Otherwise it would be inexplicable that

115

a photo dealer, who was clever enough to secure the sole rights of selling his wares in the park up to 1972, sells up to 1,000 color films each Sunday. His little counter is as much the centre of activities as the ice-cream parlor next door. People who have run out of color film queue up, with their change ready, spurred on by their photographic obsession.

And then, they shoot general views as far as the clusters of tourists permit. I have even watched one who could not penetrate to the front row hold his camera above the heads, taking pot shots, for good luck, in the general direction of the flowers.

It is no sign of photographic snobbery if we decide to put our camera away in such a situation; or make a virtue of necessity, and take only photographs of the people acting in such a strange manner. Naturally, there are also quiet days during this fine display of flowers. During weekdays the stream of visitors becomes a trickle, and we can work without disturbance, but these precious and pleasurable hours should not only be spent on experiments which with others before us have been failures: experiments such as taking pictures of the apparently limitless expanse, stretching almost to the horizon, of the fields of blossom. Certainly there are some days – they are, however, few and far between – when the dome of the sky with broken-up cloud formations stretches across the flowering fields, promising by itself a worthwhile picture. If in addition you have found a raised standpoint – already something rather unusual in the Low Countries – you will be able to obtain some impressive pictures thanks to the vast, homogeneous areas of color.

How fortunate the birds are, circling with jubilant song above all this beauty. From their view – or that of a helicopter – we should most probably be able to get ideal pictures! As it is, we have in most instances to be content with an angle of view lacking the oblique or downward approach so essential in this case. So only a very small proportion of our color film should be used for the large fields.

Close-ups instead of general views

The closer we approach our general views the better the chance of success. A few rows of flowers, diagonally cutting across the picture, will have a far more impressive and convincing effect than those pictures extending to the horizon. Or only a few flowers, maybe only a single flower, large in the picture – this is the photographer's conception!

Now we come up against the limits of the camera range. Without a near-focusing device or supplementary front lens we cannot deal with distances below three feet. If you have such accessories with you, when taking only a single flower filling your picture you have to stop down a good deal, otherwise your depth of field will not be sufficient. Stopping down, however, means long exposure times – this is where the gremlin of movement – camera-shake or subject – begins to play tricks! Moreover, flowers on the stem outdoors are almost never really still. The whole problem is indeed a subject apart and so interesting that I shall treat it in more detail on p. 164.

Perhaps you will understand me fully only after you have made the experiments yourself. Photograph a general view of a mass of flowers, and then, on the same film, a close-up picture; then project both types of view, which you can, of course, vary at will, directly one after the other. I bet that you, too, will find the close-ups more satisfying!

Well, what is valid for flowers can equally be applied to other subjects. Above all where masses of people are concerned. Admittedly a bird's-eye view, from a tower or a rooftop, of the milling crowd on the market square can be very attractive. The round, colorful umbrellas above the vegetable stalls form quiet islands in the motley of colors and shapes. However, you will be at least as successful if you descend from your vantage point and, at close quarters (about 3 to 6 feet) isolate individual scenes. For proximity creates large areas of color in place of a gaudy patchiness.

We really should make it our habit to proceed from the close-up picture to the general view instead of the other way round. Take our near subjects first, and go back step by step afterwards. Even during the preliminary judgment of the scene it is better to choose an exaggeratedly close viewpoint at first, and to increase the distance slowly after. I often did this successfully, and in most such cases I noticed that very soon I stopped because every additional feature in the picture tended to spoil it.

If, nevertheless, the restfulness of a picture is destroyed by a disturbing background, there are two alternatives to restore it. Either we restrict the zone of sharpness present by as large an aperture as possible and close-focusing of the lens, thereby throwing the background out of focus. Or we look for a different camera viewpoint. Sometimes it will be a view from above, sometimes the camera direction will be decidedly from below. Here, the blue sky can work wonders as a neutral, large-size backdrop.

Let me once more return to the subject of the successful close-up picture; there are two different types of close-up. Fruit and vegetable markets with many stalls, taken as general views, are often unfor-

tunately very disappointing as subjects. Even if we step nearer, looking at only one stall with our eyes and viewfinder, we cannot yet be sure that the restless impression has been cured.

I experienced something like this on a sunny morning at Merano, when I took a picture there. The shopwindow which delighted my eyes displayed veritable cascades of juicy fruit. The row of polished, shiny apples and bunches of grapes sparkling in oblique *contre-jour* light were only a fraction of this gorgeous sight. I did everything possible to match visual impression and photographic expression, but I simply did not succeed. I stepped closer still, and, lo and behold! the less there was in the picture, and the more temptingly the fruit grew in size in my viewfinder, the more convincing became the subject. Thus, in this instance, a distance of 9 feet from the fruit represented a general view, and only the still life "pulled in" from 5 feet with a tele-lens conveyed the impression of plenty, paradox as it may sound. As so often, here, too, the Latin phrase "pars pro toto" hits the nail on the head; freely translated it means: "a part expressing the whole thing."

After all this, you may have gained the impression that the close-up picture alone is the best approach for color photography. No, not always, but very often.

But you need not think that you ought to leave all long-distance subjects alone during your trips and rambles. It would indeed be ridiculous only to be able to point one's camera at daisies by the wayside in the face of wonderful panoramas. If you like the lighting, and the haze so often prevalent does not reduce the distant features to a flat stage-background only, you should not allow yourself to be deterred from having a look round. Maybe a suitable foreground will break up the sometimes empty expanses of sky and meadows. Perhaps a light footpath will wind its way into the background or a large storm-swept tree offer a suitable frame. The more you have enquired into the reasons for the appeal of close-up pictures in the past, the more easily will you find the means of establishing a harmonious relationship between nearness and distance. In this context I have a few more suggestions on the tip of my tongue, but I would rather reserve them for the subject of "landscapes".

However, since we are already in the mountains, flowers blossom even in an Alpine meadow. Generally we must not pick them – with the camera, however, we should! The intensely blue gentian, the Alpine roses, perhaps even the very rare Edelweiss. Do take your rucksack off for a short while and take your time. For good pictures are born of a leisurely mood.

Then you will hear the crickets chirp, feel the soft summer breeze and will become part of the great stillness. Isn't this the climax of a holiday?

Background, in or out of focus

In black-and-white photography we find pictures which are absolutely sharp from the front to the back. Others, again, show still recognizable background features which, however, are of minor importance. (It also depends on whether they consist of an ugly smoking factory chimney or the Campanile at Venice, soaring into the blue sky.) Often an out-of-focus background is used in black-and-white photography as a deliberate means of pictorial expression. It helps to "dilute" the picture. With color the situation is different.

Every pictorially important feature ought to be included in the depth-of-field zone. If the background is unimportant or, worse still, disturbing, we ought to make it invisible. This is most conveniently and also most effectively done by changing the camera position; the background is simply "submerged" and the sky placed behind the subject as ideal

backdrop. Another possibility – the photograph is taken at the largest possible aperture, near-distance setting, and with the subject filling much of the film area, when forms and outlines in the background will be strongly diffused.

The reason why half-sharp, just recognizable images are so undesirable is that subconsciously we expect a more faithful reproduction from the color photograph than from the black-and-white picture.

What we can call "artistic diffusion" in black-and-white is often merely an eye strain in the color photograph. The black-and-white picture, because it is unrealistic being without natural colors, excites the viewer's imagination. On the other hand, realism is expected in the color photograph; and our eye refuses to accept a slight unsharpness as natural!

How, then, can we avoid this trap? Well, simply like this. If we take our subject close-up with a large stop, and in pin-sharp focus with a completely out-of-focus background, the unbiassed viewer will nod his head in assent and be well satisfied. Hence, if foreground and background are to be separated, it should be done in the color photograph by extreme sharpness in front and complete unsharpness in the distance. (Look for this feature closely in the picture on p. 70.) The other solution consists of depth of field throughout the picture space. This is, however, not always simple. Certainly, the increased speed of the color film makes it easier to work with small stops and thus to enlarge the depth-of-field zone (please never confuse this sharpness in depth which is increased by stopping down, that is the depth of field, with the general image sharpness right into the corners of the picture area produced by a good quality lens!)

Sharpness throughout the picture space

Even miniature color photography did not find it easy at the beginning to fulfil the requirement of sharpness throughout the picture space. When Agfacolor film still had a speed of only ASA 4, f/8 or f/11 was scarcely possible without a tripod, even in brilliant sunlight. If, to-day, we see somebody operate with a large camera and tripod in spite of good lighting conditions, he certainly does not do this just because he is an "old-timer". Rather, the larger camera size demands a longer focal length; and the longer the focal length, the shallower the depth-of-field zone. What we Leica-people with our standard

121

ON THE FLEA MARKET, PARIS

Elsewhere in this book I mentioned that the best flash pictures really are those in which the use of flash cannot be detected at all – at least not a first sight!

Here, flash was used, of course, but the "artificial sun" of my Hobby Electronic flash blended in with the general lighting so well, that the little trick only becomes apparent after close scrutiny of the lighting conditions. You do see, don't you, that obviously the sunlight entered this little antique shop obliquely from the back. The many-colored china figures in the foreground – I would rather not vouch for their artistic value – therefore stand in the shade, or their illumination is so harsh that the rendering of their colors without the aid of flash would have been a matter of conjecture.

I therefore tried to "lift" the harsh shadows a little into the light, without, however, "plastering" them so that the contre-jour character would have been completely lost. I readily admit that this is not as simple as it looks. Welcome as the increased light intensity of the Hobby-Flash unit may be, it easily leads to "too much of a good thing" with such delicate pictures.

The full flash from a distance of 2–3 yards would thus have been too strong, while my exposure meter told me to use f/8 and $^1/_{50}$ second. I therefore set my flash unit at "half power", reducing the luminous intensity of the flash approximately by one half. This deliberate reduction of the flash, which can be carried even further by setting the flash reflector at the wide-angle position, gives the daylight pictures only a small dose of light which in the majority of cases is amply sufficient to soften the harshness of the illumination considerably.

Leica, 50 mm. Summicron, f/8, $^1/_{50}$ second, Hobby Automatic with ohne flash lamp on the camera, July.

DUTCH FOLK COSTUME FROM VOLENDAM

To begin with, I must tell you that this portrait from the picturesque little Dutch town of Volendam on the Zuider Zee was not taken in a photographer's studio.

On a dull November Sunday I met the family of a Volendam fisherman having tea in their front parlour, mother and daughter still wearing the old, enchanting folk costume. I was lucky to have brought my electronic flash along in order to be ready for anything, because the available daylight was too poor to permit more than a photographic "tour de force". Outside, however, the wind blew in gusts and it rained – no weather for taking portraits.

If I had lit the young girl with only one flash lamp, frontal or obliquely frontal illumination would have been almost the only feasible proposition. However, as I had an extension flash head, I was free to abandon frontal lighting completely and to play with my lights. I could also avoid the flash coming directly from the Leica picking out the window-frame in the background.

First I removed the main light from the camera, connected it with the longer synchro-cable and flashed it into the girl's face directly from the right, hardly more than 3 feet away. A second assistant balanced on a quickly procured ladder, so that a second flash gave a delicate, oblique glancing light from the very top. Of course, this flash was a little further away, although no more than 4½ feet.

The guide number 32 of the Hobby Flash would have required f/16 with the lamp in a frontal position. However, reduction in the light intensity caused by the distribution of the light over two lamps had to be compensated by opening up one stop, i.e. by using f/11.

At any rate, I am delighted to be able to prove with a practical example that if you use an extension flash head you can do without the usually somewhat harsh and crude frontal light, and that the possibilities of varying your flash combinations are very numerous.

Leica, 90 mm. Elmar, f/11, ¹/₅₀ second, Hobby Automatic with two flash heads.

50 mm. focal length include without difficulty in our depth of field at f/4 or f/5.6, will succeed at long focal lengths only with considerably smaller stops. The result is a longer exposure time, and that means a tripod.

The man with his large plate camera, perhaps under the black cloth, has, it is true, the opportunity of examining on his ground-glass screen the extent of his depth of field during stopping down. This is also possible with single-lens reflex-cameras and the ingeniously designed Visoflex attachments for the Leica.

The depth-of-field ring

With viewfinder cameras of "good breeding" we cannot see this depth of field. So they have a depth-of-field ring on their lens mounts. Many an amateur has taken photographs with one of these cameras for years, without understanding this very simple and streamlined table. If only he had taken five minutes to study the matter, he would realize how easily (honestly!) this gadget is operated. The identical row of stop numbers is found on either side of the index mark of the focusing scale. Suppose we are working at f/5.6, then the distance shown on the focusing scale between these two f/5.6 "markings" is the depth of field. Already you have determined the zone of sharpness appropriate for the chosen stop number. Pick up your own camera and try it! Between you and me the whole thing is an excellent substitute for a groundglass screen! Once you understand it inside out, nothing can go wrong any more.

As soon as you know how to work this simple magic ring, not only will you take your photographs more quickly, with more assurance – but also more economically. For you know at a glance everything that will still appear sharp in front of and behind the point you want to focus on. Following the trend of automation, lenses have already been designed with an automatic depth-of-field indication for any given setting. Two red pointers move over the distance scale, indicating the zone within which the picture will be sharp.

However, experience has shown that these depth-of-field indications are a little pessimistic. In practice, you think you find features in your photographs sharp which in theory lie already outside the depth of field. In addition, lenses of the same focal length but of different make and type show a different transition to unsharpness at a given stop. With some designs the sharp image abruptly "snaps" into unsharpness, with others the transition from sharpness to unsharpness occurs gradually and far more smoothly. It is all very much a matter of temperament, and dentists seem to offer an apt comparison – some drill with slow malice, while others apply determined force.

However, let us remember that due to their short focal length normal miniature lenses inherently have a large depth of field, so that the demand for sharpness throughout the picture space can really be easily met in the color photograph. With a 50 mm. lens, for example, you can in fact obtain sharpness from almost 15 feet to infinity at f/8.

Disturbing depth of field

On the other hand, however, such a favorable relation between focal length and aperture means that sometimes we may have a certain amount of difficulty in fulfilling the opposite of our two alternatives, that is the total obliteration of the background. For even if our depth-of-field ring promises us sharp reproduction only up to 24 or 30 feet, the background and even the far distance will still be recognizable, and so there may be disturbing features.

In such cases we can employ the following, quite different solutions: –

1. We look, if possible, for a different camera position, kneel down or even lie on the ground, thus placing our subject against the sky or some other neutral area.

Or, we mount some raised object, such as a stool, table, ladder, a hill, or the like, because this cuts the background off and produces a clear, restful, and sharp rendering of the middle ground, street, earth, or meadow.

2. We deliberately choose a large aperture, the larger the better, shortening the exposure time, of course, to compensate for it. When focusing on very near subjects, heads, or "head-and-shoulders" (apologies, but I simply must place this monster word in quotation marks!) we will succeed in eliminating the background more or less completely.

3. We resort to longer focal lengths! "Ha", some readers may think at this stage, "now he is letting the cat out of the bag! This chapter I am going to ignore, because my lens is not interchangeable!"

However, I would ask you to follow me just a little longer! I admit that taking photographs with interchangeable lenses is not an essential part of a guide-book to color photography, but this particular book would be unthinkable without it; in a moment I shall tell you why.

Detachment from the background

We know now that in color photography compromises with background definition are not readily accepted. We have also learned that the "built-in" large depth of field of the normal miniature lenses can only be sufficiently decreased by the use of large apertures, so that background contours are effectively repressed.

However, this situation changes at once as soon as we fall back on a longer focal length. The interest among ambitious amateurs in cameras with interchangeable lenses increases continuously. Unfortunately, many camera fans have no clear idea of all that can be achieved with various focal lengths. Even the proud owners of an additional focal length lens hardly know more about their long-focus lens than that they can "pull in the distance" with it. Or they use it in order to reproduce their subjects large from short distances.

This is the reason why the longer focal length lenses are called portrait lenses and the wide angle types architectural lenses. These terms, however, only signify part of their characteristic tasks.

It is very well known that the depth of field decreases rapidly with longer focal length – and *vice versa*. If a large depth of field becomes necessary with long focal lengths, we will soon be faced with the necessity of using a tripod. Please bear in mind that an exposure of f/5.6 and $^1/_{125}$ second demands as much as $^1/_{15}$ second at f/16! This difficulty is sometimes reached very quickly with long focal lengths. At $^1/_{15}$ second handheld – well, have you ever tried it?

On the other hand, the problem can also be argued from the opposite direction. The shallow depth of field is a blessing when a foreground subject only is the main feature, and the background not required in the picture. Thus with deliberate short-distance focusing and full aperture we will obtain such small depths of field that a pleasing detachment from the background takes place. This goes so far that the fast lenses compel us to take great care during focusing in order to set the correct distance in view of the narrow zone of sharpness. For, if we focus only one or two inches too far back, or on the face generally, the tip of the nose will become woolly and unsharp.

These are extreme examples of short-distance setting of 3 to 5 feet at full aperture. If the subjects are further away, we will have a quite useable zone of sharpness. But it remains true that the long focal length allows us to manipulate depth of field far more effectively, and our difficulties with the background are much reduced compared with the short focal length.

Moreover, a longer focal length also has a narrower angle of view. You exclude the background, as it were, and thus require a smaller area to represent it. Sometimes a slight turn of your camera is enough to make use of the even, light, and neutral surface of a wall, of a dark hedge, or of a deeper shadow. If even this is impossible, you must try to suppress the effect of disturbing color areas still visible in the background by reducing even further the distance of the features in the foreground, because the larger the pictorially essential factors are shown, the easier will the background be overlooked.

When we look through the camera viewfinder, which naturally can only show the picture frame of the changed focal length, but not the decreased depth of field, we must develop some imagination and make use of our experience. The call for a ground-glass screen and reflex camera is therefore quite understandable with longer focal lengths because it facilitates the judgment of the pictorial effect. Hence, an increasing number of Leica amateurs adopt the mirror housings, called Visoflex housings, for they combine the advantages of the miniature camera with the convenience of the ground-glass screen image. In the meantime, the introduction of the Visoflex II housing has made it possible to use the smaller 90 mm. tele-lens with the reflex housing. Since this focal length which has now been reinforced with a faster lens (90 mm. Summicron f/2) calls for a particularly accurate observation of the depth-of-field zone in portraits and a variety of close-up subjects, a gap felt by Leica-fans who favor the groundglass screen with longer focal lengths has been closed.

Especially during the last few months I have been able to gain much practical experience by using the 90 mm. lens alternately with the viewfinder and the new Visoflex system. Whenever I wanted to take a still subject I preferred the leisurely method of groundglass focusing. I had plenty of time. But for real snaps or children's pictures where the focusing had to follow every movement, I worked with my 90 mm. directly on the Leica again.

Envious glance at paiting

We cannot compare painting and photography. Both are based on different principles. However, if I do draw parallels once in a while, it makes me green with envy to think how freely, and how far less dependently on his tools the painter can create, in comparison with the narrow restrictions under which the photographer has to work. You only have to consider the way the painter, whether he works with a brush or a crayon, imparts his personal note even to the simplest sketch. He just leaves out whatever disturbs his subject although it lies in his field of view. He can go even further, by adding to his picture features he has seen at different times and in different places. Thus, the painter interprets.

The photographer is tied down

Poor photographer! What his viewfinder tells him is in the field of view of his lens at the moment of the exposure is recorded with accuracy and without mercy. No matter how original his own conception of the picture, he can hardly omit and just as little add anything. His pictures must be faithful records of the original.

I think I know no better example of the dependence of photography on actually existing features than the famous Spanish Steps in Rome. At their foot the traffic roars from morning till night. It would simply mean risking one's life, were one even to attempt walking to the centre of the road in order to take the magnificent sweep of the steps from there. However, having safely reached the opposite pavement, from where the angle would be ideal, one finds innumerable overhead wires feeding a fleet of trolley buses with electric current have descended into the picture area. No matter how good the lighting and impressive the clouds in the sky crowning the whole, there will be disappointment; everything is surmounted by an ugly mesh of wires like the frame of an old umbrella. But even if all these wires did not exist, there would still be no moment during which the traffic stands still, leaving your foreground unadorned with passing chromium-flashing motor cars.

Naturally, there are opportunities in photography when we can really do something original. In the case of a still life, for instance, or with interiors it is often in our own hands to arrange things according to our personal wishes and tastes. In portraiture, too, we have the opportunity of directing our model, we can play around with the lighting, change the background, or again make use of a mood in order to create pictures closely corresponding to our imagination.

However, as soon as the subject is a fixed feature, our art of direction is at an end. Obviously we can push a disturbing bicycle to one side if it is parked next to the beautiful entrance of an ancient town hall. We can also, as we have already pointed out repeatedly, avoid undesirable objects by a clever choice of camera viewpoint. These are all expedients, or, better, aids. But the scenery behind our genre picture remains unchanged and cannot be influenced. Well, is this really true? If we only work with one lens rigidly mounted in our camera — yes!

Conjuring with Perspective

However, there is yet another way of influencing pictures according to our wishes. Is it not strange that this possibility, although it has existed ever since interchangeable lenses were introduced, is so little known? Even amateurs with several lenses only rarely use this opportunity.

Perhaps you will contend that the purpose of interchangeable lenses is well-known. With a tele-lens, for instance, we can obtain a section of the general field of view, pull in the distance, or represent nearby features still larger in the picture area, because with medium-long and long focal lengths we can almost extinguish the background, and the pictorially essential subject can be placed in the picture space without any disturbing detail. You have only to remember the many good landscape photographs which only became possible by rendering the mountains large in the picture by, as it were, jumping across the valleys. Or remember usually extremely difficult color photographs of high, brilliant stained-glass windows in churches, which, taken through a tele-lens, can fill the entire picture area, while through a normal lens they would be no more than little splotches of color in the general darkness of the interior; not to mention the convergence of verticals to which the shorter focal lengths are prone on such occasions.

Yes, certainly, we all know about these things.

On the other hand it is largely unknown that we can also strongly influence the apparent perspective effect of a picture according to whether we use a wide angle, a standard, or a tele-lens. In other words, it is possible after all to "move" subjects, which are obviously immovable, according to our wishes. We can soften the rigidity of the conventional rendering and modify the proportions according to their importance. We can reproduce the foreground large and reduce the background to insignificance. Or, conversely, deliberately render the foreground smaller and have the background dominate the picture completely. And all this with the aid of interchangeable lenses of varying focal lengths!

At any rate, this teaches us the following facts:

If the foreground has the right proportions and occupies in our picture the dimensions we had anticipated for it, while the background plays more or less the part of a frame or backdrop only, a picture taken with a standard lens will probably satisfy us. All we have to do is to see to the correct camera position, so that nothing in the background grows out of somebody's head, or other intersections disturb the harmony. But if foreground and background are equally essential to the picture, there is only the one possibility of moving the foreground closer to the background. People can change their standpoint, fixed objects such as houses, trees, and son cannot.

The background becomes larger

Here we have "conjuring with perspective". Using our tele-lens we step back until the foreground appears at the same size in the view-finder, in spite of the long focal length of our lens, as during the setting with the normal focal length. The distant subject appears closer and is reproduced larger.

Even with a 90 mm. lens in place of the 50 mm., by this trick the background will be reproduced at almost twice its original size. How-

133

ever, with a focal length of 135 mm., the dimensions of the pulled-in background will be almost trebled, and be exactly four times with a 200 mm. lens, such as the famous Telyt for the Leica. In this case, our distance from the foreground, if it is to be reproduced at constant size, will be, for example, 20 yards instead of 5 yards with the normal lens.

In many cases, therefore, a longer focal length is a suitable means of producing better, more impressive pictures by a deliberately larger rendering of the background compared with a normal-sized foreground.

Believe me, dear friends, this possibility is downright exciting once we have grasped its significance! Only then will the purchase of a larger focal length lens be really worth-while. And it will also pay to think about what further consequences will result from this juggling with interchangeable lenses.

We want the background smaller

There are, however, opposite cases too. Let us assume the background as taken with the normal lens is too large. We would not like to miss it altogether because after all, it shows where we are, but the foreground should more or less dominate the whole picture.

We then approach the desired foreground very closely with a shorter focal length, that is a wide-angle lens, so that it appears in the picture at the same size as if it were taken with a standard lens. The background will thereby be automatically reduced in size!

This case in which we wish to make the background appear smaller on purpose occurs quite frequently. Often the background is overpowering, without our being able to make it disappear. This is where the change in the proportions – lange, emphasized foreground – small, subsidiary background will be a welcome method of improving pictorial composition.

The foreground becomes smaller

What do you do, for instance, if the background appears large enough even with a normal lens, but the foreground seems far too prominent and dominating in front of it? Imagine yourself standing in a wide valley in front of a church, where the spire, dominating everything, soars into the sky, while the neighbouring mountains, although large enough, do not really look as prominent as they ought to. (Perhaps your standpoint is too far down the valley, that is your view is wrong.) If you want to improve matters by taking up a position further to the back, such as on a nearby hill, the church will, indeed, look smaller, but so will the mountains in the background. However, if you go back with a long focal length lens (the longer the focal length the better!) far enough until the mountains in the background are again as large as they were before with the standard lens, the church will now fit in with its surroundings instead of dominating them.

If the background has the desired size, but the foreground is to be reduced and subdued, we use a longer focal length, walking away from the background until it assumes the same size again as with the standard lens. This automatically reduces the foreground.

Perhaps amateurs that have "arrived" will tell me now that all this has been well known for a long time. As a matter of fact, the late Dr. W. Grabner drew our attention to this conjuring with perspective in a short, far too little known, pamphlet more than 20 years ago.

I would not like to conclude this conjuring session without making the following point: – It is common knowledge that the shorter focal length results in a wider angle of view. Expressed in numerical values, a standard lens, e. g. of 50 mm. focal length, has an angle of view of 46°, the shorter 35 mm. focal length already as much as 64°, while the new 21 mm. super-wide angle (21 mm. Angulon f/5.6) even offers an angle of view of 92°!

It is obvious that we must work with the shorter focal length if the angle of view of the normal lens is no longer sufficient and there is no possibility of obtaining a picture by increasing the distance between camera and object. This is a very frequent experience when traveling, and having to miss the picture is sometimes very sad. For interiors, a short focal length is indeed an absolute must. But I must warn you against doing too much of a good thing by calling in the super-wide angle, omitting the 35 mm. lens. It is true that with the 21 mm. focal length the coverage of the camera is astonishingly wide from a close distance, however, the extreme shortness of the focal length demands very meticulous work with the camera because the slightest tilt makes the verticals converge, while in the hands of a layman perspective distortion can assume downright grotesque forms.

A wide-angle lens of 35 mm. focal length continues to be much more useful for amateur purposes; it must be stressed as a particularly attractive feature that its speed has lately been increased to f/2 in the new Summicron, so that it has become a real rival of the fast 50 mm. lens.

The Make-believe Lens

In connection with the exaggerated perspective of wide-angle pictures there comes to my mind a story, half annoying, half amusing, concerning the wide-angle lens. Many years ago I took my family to a holiday resort, attracted by the profusely illustrated prospectus of a *pension* in the mountains. Our imagination ran riot as we studied the excellent photographs. They not only showed an attractive, white house, with large trees in front of it, but also views of a spacious garden with a fountain in a small pond; deck chairs inviting us to rest were generously spaced out; a park promising peace and quiet, and privacy from other guests.

The interior of the guest house, too, appeared no less generous and spacious in its proportions. A hall with a reading room, a palatial dining hall, and a winter garden in which one could almost take a walk. The place was the very thing for us.

When we arrived – to make matters worse it was raining cats and dogs – everything was different and a big disappointment. It appeared to me as if I had returned, after many years, to the haunts of my childhood, where one remembers everything much larger than it is in reality. Not only were the rooms tiny; the dining hall was narrow, too. About the park I would rather say nothing at all, it was no more than on outsize allotment, with a little pool in the centre instead of a pond.

What had happened? The perspective rendering of the pictures did not correspond to the natural impression, because they had been taken with an extreme wide-angle lens. I had frequent occasion to think of this example in later years whenever I wanted to exaggerate the feeling of space in a picture in the interest of its general impression. Ever since, my wife has dubbed the wide-angle lens the "make-believe" lens.

Cleverly taken advertising shots are based on this effect. What does the owner of a small factory do if he wants to impress his customers a little with "views of our works?" He shows us vast halls with machinery and lathes, an exterior front losing itself in the far distance, everything betraying a dynamic spirit and enterprise. All these are, of course, merely views taken with an ultra-wide angle lens, which makes a strong impression on anyone not familiar with photography. All you have to do is to count the windows in the building receding rapidly into the background, in order to be "in the picture". A forgery? Hardly. Rather, magic with the focal length.

Which focal length first?

In the face of so many examples I hope I have convinced the amateur of the effect of interchangeable optics. Logically he will now want to know how to go about extending his equipment in the direction of the "camera system":

Whether the right thing to do is to buy a wide-angle lens or a longer focal length after all?

I am sure not everyone will have either the enterprise or the cash of the American photo enthusiast at Kansas City who, on the morning after one of my lectures, surprised his photo dealer with the impatient words. "I should like to buy the whole equipment and all those lenses with which this fellow works"!

I believe the first step to enlarge your scope should be the purchase of a lens of longer focal length. This does not mean that you should go too far, deciding on an extremely long focal length. It is better to take that lens with which you become familiar most quickly. For a Leica man, then, this would be the 90 mm. Elmar, Elmarit or Summicron. Of course it could also be the 135 mm. Hektor, but in this case you will often miss the intermediate focal length which in my opinion is called for more frequently. Moreover, the danger of camera-shake is less with the 90 mm. than with the 135 mm. You should bear in mind that the longer the focal length, the more critical the danger of camera-shake.

Once you have learned to work with the long focal length lens, the next addition should be a wide-angle, and it is preferable not to jump immediately to the ultra-wide angle but to the 35 mm. Summaron or Summicron instead. Incidentally, experienced photographers confirm almost unanimously that apart from exceptional cases, the order of the most frequent use of their various focal lengths is roughly as follows:

1. Standard focal length 50 mm.
2. Longer focal length 90 mm.
3. Short focal length 35 mm.
4. Long focal length 135 mm.
5. Ultra short focal length 28 mm.
6. Ultra long focal length 200 mm.

Due to the recently introduced 35 mm. Summicron f/2 wide-angle lens the picture may, however, change in time in so far as many Leica fans have begun to do without the normal focal length altogether and to promote the shorter 35 mm. lens to the role of standard lens. If you handle it with skill and do not attempt to photograph portraits, you will be able to avoid the impression of perspective distortion and come to appreciate the advantage of greater depth of field even with large apertures.

138

Whenever I go out without specific photographic intentions I always put the 35 mm. wide-angle on my Leica, just for luck. I must stress, however, that I always carry my camera with me, practically day and night, or at least have it within reasonable distance, whether weather conditions are favorable or not.

If time permits me to look around for photographic subjects, I take along the 90 mm. in a special leather container, so that I am prepared for any event and not only for taking the occasional portrait, but also scenes impossible to approach closely with the short focal length. It then happens as a matter of course that I am all of a sudden faced with a situation calling for a third focal length, such as the normal 50 mm. or the ultra short 21 mm. focal length.

On photo-journeys when everything, even leisure, is sacrificed to the hunt for the picture I have the entire range of lenses from 21 mm. to 200 mm. at hand; nevertheless, here, too, my equipment goes into two bags kept rigidly apart, because the weight of two bags for any length of time is apt to become a little discouraging. If you have a companion, this problem, too, can of course be solved.

The first bag takes the Leica with the wide-angle lens. If you own an M 2, you will have a built-in viewfinder, but I push a special wide-angle viewfinder onto the camera, although I admit that in the case of the divided equipment under discussion it would be better to take the M 2 as the taking camera since it also indicates the fields of view for 50 mm. and 90 mm.

The longest lens contained in this bag is the 90 mm. A UV filter is screwed into the front of each lens (see p. 92), also, generously, each has its own lens hood, which, as you know, is turned round when not in use and so does not take up any additional space. Then there is room for several films (5 cassettes), the exposure meter, the intriguing, although rarely-used, polar filter (see p. 92) und pieces of chamois leather and dusting brushes.

A neck-strap is fixed to the eyes of the Leica so that it can occasionally be carried round the neck outside the large bag. That is really all.

If you go in for many close-ups of subjects often less than 3 ft. away you will be well advised to take the very handy near-focusing device along; this, as we all know, connects with the wonderful 50 mm. dual-

GOLDEN GATE BRIDGE AT SAN FRANCISCO

I do not claim that this picture is the incarnation of America. However, if with half a dozen or a dozen pictures you want to convey a typical impression of the phenomenon that is America, the series will be incomplete unless the Golden Gate Bridge is included. The bridge spans the Golden Gate, the bay of San Francisco. It is a symbol of the optimism and drive of the citizens of the New World and of the achievements of their engineers. (It is perhaps surpassed by the grand view of New York's skyline seen from the Hudson River.)

Many photographs have been taken of Golden Gate Bridge. Most of them show this wonder of twentieth-century civil engineering in its surroundings, as a connecting link between the two high banks on either side of the city.

However, I conceived the idea of photographing the bridge in complete isolation. I wanted to show the elastic strength of the concrete ribbon suspended, as it were, from giant spider's threads, carrying six lanes of traffic. I imagined that it must look fantastic from above, if the camera could be pointed from one of the pylons of the bridge at the depths of the blue-green water. Don't ask me how I got up there! The special permission necessary was easy to obtain. Again and again I was amazed as well as pleased at the helpfulness of the Americans, (even of their authorities). A short phone-call, a handshake – okay! There is an elevator but not for sightseeing tourists, only for the maintenance workers: a narrow, dark iron cask, recalling notions of submarines.

But it is worth-while: – the view from the top is breathtaking and makes you dizzy. Photographically the impression is enhanced by the use of a wide-angle lens, because it makes depth appear even deeper.

Leica, 35 mm, Summaron, f/11, ¹/₁₀₀ second, April, 3 p.m., sunlight.

ICE FLOES ON THE ELBE NEAR HAMBURG

Such hard winters are a pleasingly rare occurrence. On the great rivers the ice is packed so close that one can almost comfortably walk from one bank to the other.

It is Saturday afternoon. These children from Hamburg are having fun on the ice, jumping, some frightened, some with daring, from floe to floe.

The weather is hazy, although the sun has managed to struggle through a little and to light up the foreground in relief. But the background only just reveals the contours of the "Deutsche Werft" shipyards, the distance looks even more distant when it is veiled in a delicate blue.

Although the horizon runs almost through the middle of the picture (which is usually unfavourable), this photograph is balanced by the large "tub", the ocean-going freighter which slowly appears from the distance crashing its way through the ice. This ship is the absolute centre of attention, unfailingly attracting the eye.

With such and similar subjects you should try always to get the human element unobtrusively into the picture. This gives a measure of comparison between the dimensions of the individual picture elements. Also, the colorful clothing brings more life into the color photograph. Here, too, the rule that red can always be used to advantage in the foreground is a great help.

Leica, 50 mm. Summicron, f/5.6, ¹/₅₀ second, January, 3 p. m., weak sun.

range Summicron by a single push. This near-focusing device, whose tiny "spectacles", placed over the field windows of viewfinder and rangefinder, work parallax-free, permits an approach to the subject down to 19". Close-up shots of this kind are possible out of hand without difficulty.

Second Bag for Tele-days

The second bag, then, contains everything I need for my work with longer focal lengths. Ready for action is the new Visoflex II with the angle-prism focusing magnifier through which the upright and right-way-round groundglass image is viewed. It has an adapter ring screwed in which in turn takes the head of my 90 mm. lens housed in Bag No. 1. The 135 mm. Hektor with a short focusing mount for the Visoflex also takes up little space, and it has a lens hood of its own so that I need not swap the same lens hood between the 90 mm. and 135 mm. lenses when I am in a hurry. Finally, there is the 200 mm. Telyt, also with its lens hood at the ready in spite of the larger space it needs. Because when you are rushed any screwing and turning means loss of time.

This of course also raises the question whether the camera for long and extremely long focal lengths should be carried in another bag or not. Well, I have made it a habit to carry a second one in my tele-bag – you will be surprised to learn it is a veteran model from pre-war days, with the slow speeds built in afterwards; after all, neither rangefinder, viewfinder nor the very convenient bayonet fitting for the lens change are needed with the groundglass focusing on the Visoflex mirror housing. The latter is screwed in position once and for all, and the camera behind it can just as well be a basic, simple Leica.

This little chapter is headed "For Tele-days", because I would not dream of always burdening myself with my second bag; when I am traveling it is either left in my hotel bedroom or in my automobile, while I go picture-hunting with Bag No. 1 with the shorter 35, 50, and 90 mm. lenses.

But as soon as I have become more familiar with my surroundings having made mental notes of favorable photographic possibilities here and there the second bag comes into its own. One can even go so far as to set an exclusive tele-day aside, when opportunities for unforeseen snapshots will be strictly ignored while the hunt is on for tele-subjects alone. The choice of motif will then be entirely different.

144

Here is an admission: Without a sturdy tripod, a tele-day may end with a lot of disappointing results. It will always be part of my luggage on such occasions, because I am often forced to stop down so much that even with a 40 ASA film exposure times in the region of $1/50$, $1/25$ second or even longer are necessary.

Naturally, you can also carry your entire equipment all in one bag, like a traveler in photographic goods; but I am afraid that this will often be something of a handicap, because it will make your photographic activities too conspicuous as well as too cumbersome.

Flash ... in daylight

I am deliberately mentioning flash in daylight first, for I think more highly of supplementary daylight flash than of the often indifferent results of flash by night – at least in the case of the color transparencies.

True, most flashes, whether the small flashbulbs or the ingenious electronic flash – more economical in the long run – are fired in pitch-darkness. This is ancient photographic tradition. Our fathers burned their fingers on flash powder, while our mothers took their curtains down for fear of fires.

But let us talk about color, particularly with color reversal film. We are sufficiently familiar with the accurate exposure time required. Its exposure latitude is not very remarkable, and it therefore does not take particularly kindly to very contrasty lighting.

Nevertheless have encouraged you not to shun side light during the day, nor to avoid back-lighting. But I have always made a point of drawing your attention to the fact that you had to reckon with darkened colors in the shadow parts of the picture as well as with color reflections from neighboring objects.

Also, since we are allowed to do anything but expose for the dark portions of our subjects, as this would cause a washing-out of the highlights with strong contrast, we have in many cases to fall back on the aid of supplementary light, either from white sheets and other reflecting media or from supplementary flash.

It is sad, but true, that very few people dare to use flash in daylight. Not because the color of the flashlight is wrong, for we can use special blue-tinted flashbulbs, while electronic flash is in any case suitable for daylight color film and can claim the distinction of being a substitute for sunlight.

A convenient method

Most of us are simply a little scared of the technique of having to calculate the stop number with the aid of the so-called guide-number or flash factor. I shall explain how to use this guide number quite simply in the chapter "Flash by Night". During the day, however, we can get along without arithmetic altogether, firing our flash "at point-blank range" as it were.

This means you first find out how you would expose your subject if no supplementary flash were available.

Since the main purpose of supplementary daylight flash consists of an effective softening of the shadows, you can naturally disregard the shadows entirely for the exposure determination. Rather, you should make a point of measuring the high-light portions of the picture, be it a sunlit landscape in the background or other areas lighter than the shadows.

This gives you the certainty that the color rendering of the light part of the picture is not upset by over-exposure. For softening the shadows with your flash you might adopt the following very simple method based on my experiences with the Braun Hobby Automatic and Agfacolor CT 18, which has an index of 50 for ASA-calibrated exposure meters.

> Approximately f/11 up to 7' flash distance.
>
> Approximately f/8 up to 10' flash distance.
>
> Approximately f/5.6 up to 14' flash distance.
>
> Approximately f/4 up to 17' flash distance.

If Kodachrome is used it is necessary to use one stop larger aperture.

(For the Hobby Special or F 60 one half stop or one and one half stop larger should be chosen for the flash distances given.) Of course, a flash effect can be achieved in daylight even beyond a range of 17', but this involves quite large apertures and therefore very short shutter speeds. (However, with focal plane shutters speeds above $1/50$ second are taboo with electronic flash, a fact about which I shall have to say more shortly.)

We must bear in mind that exposure with electronic flash is always controlled with the iris diaphragm instead of the shutter speed. The reason for this is the very short duration of the electronic flash – $1/1000$ second in the Hobby. Whether we set our between-lens shutter at $1/60$, $1/125$, or even $1/250$ second, the flash is faster still, jumping, as it were, into the time during which the shutter is open; provided, of course, that the camera is designed for the use of flash units. It will then be equipped with a so-called synchronised shutter which, on opening, makes a firing contact that triggers the flash.

While blade-type or "compur" shutters can be set at will, cameras fitted with focal-plane shutters, which include the Leica, must not be set at speeds shorter than $1/50$ second with electronic flash. Otherwise only part of the negative will be exposed to the flash. The explanation of this is that in cameras with focal-plane shutters the exposure is effected by the movement of two roller blinds. A slit of adjustable width passes across the film, exposing it to the light. The shorter the exposure time required, the narrower this slit is set. As soon as this becomes narrower than the film width of 36 mm., it can naturally only transmit the light for part of its way across the film during the $1/1000$ second of the duration of the electronic flash.

In the current Leica Models the movement of the two shutter curtains is arranged so that the electronic flash just illuminates the entire negative area during $1/50$ second. In the case of older cameras with focal-plane shutter the minimum is generally no more than $1/25$ or $1/30$ second. Hence we must be a little careful when using combined daylight and electronic flash lest our subjects move too quickly and restrict our flash photography to the less temperamental among them.

Nor, if we are forced to use relatively long exposure times, must we open up our stop too far, in order to avoid over-exposure of our color film. Therefore, the combination of aperture stop and shutter speed must always be chosen as if no flash at all were used.

I am going to show you a typical example in order to explain to you as clearly as possible the use of supplementary daylight flash (with Compur- as well as focal-plane shutters).

You are about to take a back-lighted daylight portrait on a balcony, and your sitter looks into the shadow. This is often really the only method of obtaining faces without dazzle and the resulting squint. Let us assume you obtain an exposure meter reading – please remember not to take too much notice of the deep shadow parts – of $1/125$ second at f/8 or $1/60$ second at f/11 which, as we all know, is the same.

If now you took your picture without flash – and other reflecting aids – this would result in muddy colors in the shadows and perhaps a blue reflection into the bargain. However, if you make a point of exposing for the shadows, the colors in the highlights will simply disappear. Possibly you may find, as a result of the burnt-out highlights, shoulders and hair covered with "snow", an effect you had not at all intended.

Hence you had better stick to the exposure for the light parts of your subject, bringing out the colors in the shadows by means of the flash. At subject distances of at least 7 and at most 10 feet and f/11 to f/8 you will be surprised at the color quality of your shadows.

If your portrait is full length or a whole group, you simply go back further, open your stop to f/8 or f/5.6, naturally with due allowance for this by shortening the exposure time to $^1/_{125}$ or $^1/_{250}$ second respectively (an automatic process with the light value setting). The flash will be equally efficient from 13 to 17 feet. You can let it act as a supplementary light source from the camera without difficulty.

Users of focal-plane shutters cannot be quite as generous here, because the constant exposure time demands an equally constant smaller stop. They are therefore forced to have the flash directed at the subject at a distance of approximately 7 to 10 feet while retreating further back with the camera only. (Extension cables to enable the camera to fire the flash in such cases are available.)

What I have told you now is merely "first aid" with flash for subjects in strong contrast back-light, in unfriendly weather, or during daytime in rooms without sun.

Of course, one immediately and invariably sees that flash has been responsible for at least half of such pictures. However, I soundly dislike pictures betraying at first sight the use of this lighting expedient. In my opinion, those flash photographs are best in which the flash is entirely unnoticeable and its effect mistaken for that of the sun or quite normal reflections!

Back-lighted color pictures really ought to retain something of their "against-the-light" character! Otherwise that which is the essence of the picture's atmosphere is "flashed away".

Only a Pinch of Flashlight

At any rate, I much prefer a mere hint of flashlight, also called a "pinch" of flashlight. It does no more than pick up the shadows and their colors without falsifying the lighting character of the picture.

On the whole, the danger of too much is greater than that of too little. The light output of current flash units – the Hobby Automatic and the later, very practical and handy Hobby Special and F 60 amateur

149

units – is so strong, that some experience is needed for the successful painting of the shadows with just the right amount of flash. Your own experience is your best guide, and you will be well advised to keep records of flash distances and stops during your own experiments.

I would like to point out in this connection that the Hobby Automatic has a special button for Half-Power with an effective decrease of the lighting intensity to about 60 % of its full strength.

Flashbulbs have a longer flash duration

With flashbulbs which, as we know, are fired by small batteries, cameras with focal-plane shutters too can be used with shorter exposure times. The flash duration here is far longer than in the case of electronic flash, flooding the subject with light throughout the entire traveling time of the roller blinds. The best utilization of the flash illumination is also obtained at $1/50$ second, while, naturally, light is "cut off" with shorter exposure times. Your photo dealer will be pleased to give you further advice on this point. Various manufacturers supply flashbulbs of various lighting intensities and duration so that practically any task can be tackled.

Here, another very important point should be stressed. Since electronic flash has a far shorter firing delay than flashbulbs, synchronized cameras must correspondingly provide for the correct triggering of both types of flash. The standard sign X stands for electronic flash, and capital M for expendable flashbulbs. If you get muddled with the two settings, this will cause unpleasant surprises, because if by mistake you have set the electronic flash at "M", your flash tube has expended its light long before your shutter bestirs itself to open! I am speaking from bitter experience!

Also, you should, whenever possible, use blue-tinted flashbulbs for daylight color film. True, the clear, untinted ones will be quite useful as a supplementary light source, but they produce a very warm light which does not really mix well with daylight.

Color negative film with clear flashbulbs

Friends of negative film are well served with any type of flash. Whether they use electronic flash or clear flashbulbs, everything will be printed correctly in the color laboratory so long as you do not mix the two or use clear bulbs in daylight. The darkroom technician with his set of color filters for the negative-positive process will be particularly delighted if you offer him color negatives exposed only by flashbulbs, because the color composition of this light is ideal and demands almost no filter correction. The advantage of color negative film is that it can be used with quite high guide numbers, because the light intensity of clear flash bulbs is naturally higher than of blue-tinted ones. This is an important tip for flash illumination of large rooms.

Flash . . . by night

In the evening or at night the flash is our best aid. Also, we should now know more about the intensity of its light. It is, of course, calculated by means of the guide number.

Most of us will perhaps already be familiar with the magic formula – the guide number is divided by the distance of the flash from the subject. The result determines the stop number we have to use.

A practical example will look like this: we want to use the flash from a distance of 10 feet. Let the guide number of the flash be 55 (Hobby Automatic with daylight Kodachrome). We now calculate 55 divided by 10 = 5.5. Naturally, we can use f/5.6. Our color film will be exposed correctly if . . .

If we operate in a "normal" room. By this we mean that we give our flash the chance to attack our subject with the aid of all the reflections from light walls and the ceiling.

Of course, guide numbers are assessed by the manufacturers of flash equipment under favourable conditions. I. e. not in the coal cellar, nor in the large sports arena, where the light is not supplemented by any reflection as it is in a room.

Thus, the guide number is only valid without restriction if we use the flash, as it were, between our own four (light) walls.

Now it would be nonsensical to change the guide numbers with the varying exposure conditions for our indoor subjects, such as one guide number for the lounge with dark furniture and another for the gleaming kitchen. This would be far too confusing. Instead we only memorize one guide number, modifying the stop as the case requires; one stop larger in dark rooms with high ceilings, and at least two stops outdoors at night, i. e. f/4 instead of f/8.

151

Here, the respective advantages and drawbacks of Compur shutter and focal-plane shutter cameras become quite immaterial, because it does not matter in the least whether we expose at $^1/_{25}$ second or $^1/_{250}$ second. The only effective and valid exposure time is always the $^1/_{1000}$ second of the electronic flash duration!

Two flashes together are much better!

I am now going to pass a very critical remark on the use of flash with color film where the flash is the only light source. I do not think much of color photographs taken with frontal flash illumination. This light is too flat, too brutal for my liking, moreover, its intensity falls off far too rapidly towards the background. The results again and again confirm my view: degraded purplish-brown colors in the background, the faces light and somewhat frigid if the intensity of the flash was too great.

Naturally, there is a way, frequently used in black-and-white photography, to distribute the light a little more softly, the flash is directed against the light colored ceiling (bounce flash) if this is reasonably low, or the reflector is simply removed from behind the flash tube. However, this decreases our lighting intensity so much, that we have to open up at least two, if not three stop values.

The extension flash head is a much more efficient method. This enables us far better to play with our lights and to introduce an infinite number of lighting variations. With the Braun Hobby Automatic we can even use three flash heads – as the experts call them. Only, we cannot hold these three flash heads ourselves, we have to rely on outside help. The attraction of several flashes consists precisely in their contrast effects, so that they have to be fired from as different directions as possible.

You will find a very enlightening example on p. 123 and p. 124 with their corresponding texts. Here you can see quite clearly that several flashes result in very good modelling. Let us note the following points for the use of two Hobby flash heads:

1) The light intensity is decreased due to the splitting up of the power between two sources, even if the quality of illumination is improved. This is compensated by opening up one stop from the value obtained from the guide number.

2) The distance valid for the calculation of the guide number (guide number divided by flash distance = stop number) is always measured from the flash head nearer to the subject.

3) Obviously the two flashes should not be fired from the same direction. The effect would be scarcely different from that of a single flash. Instead, we must give pronounced side or even back-light with one of the flash heads. Invariably with this arrangement one flash should be fired closer to the subject than the other. In most cases, an assistant will do this with the extension flash head at the end of a 17 foot-cable and, therefore, with much freedom of movement. If, for instance, you work with your camera and attached flash head from

a distance of 10 feet, the extension flash head is best placed at a distance of 5 feet from the subject (distance ratio of the two lamps 1:2).

4) Very smoky rooms can cause a puzzling blue cast. To avoid this, you first open the window to let out the fog before taking flash pictures in the room. On the other hand, thick smoke behind your sitter, magically lit up from the back by the second flash, can yield surprising effects. An efficient pipe- or cigarette smoker might perhaps kneel

behind the model, producing as much smoke as his lungs will allow. Then is the time to press your button.

5) Watch your assistant with the extension flash like a hawk. Often he becomes so absorbed in what you are doing that he does not notice that his reflector points anywhere but at the subject.

6) A lens hood, as we all know, should always be used. Particularly in this case to prevent the light from a flash held to one side of the picture from sneaking into your lens unexpectedly.

7) The effect of the flash is not intensified to any marked extent any more by decreasing the flash distance below 5 feet. If you have to approach very small objects to be flashed from 3 feet or even closer distances, the guide number calculation should not be based on inches, but as if the flash distance were 5 feet. However, it is useful to know that very bright close-up objects will invariably be very successful at f/11 to f/16.

8) When taking small children and subjects which do not keep still, it is best to determine beforehand a fixed distance with your assistant and to try to keep to this distance. Therefore you should follow the movement of the object, which at the same time gives you the advantage of not having to adjust your stop every time.

The ideal case: the bathroom

Someone once wrote: "in the bathroom there are plenty of subjects ... a rich field of activity . . . with one or two photoflood lamps one could . . ." The whole thing had the title: "Where to snap our youngest?"

Whoever he was gave a very dangerous piece of advice, at a time when we did not yet have flash safely packed in bulbs or tubes!

You see, these photoflood lamps aren't really to be recommended. Not only do they bring us into conflict with the law, but also, on occasion, with 230 volts, because most bathrooms are earthed very well; the photoflood lamps not so well. A tiny loose contact, a bare wire – and you have taken your last bathroom picture (if it is not your last picture altogether!).

This is the reason why our electrical regulations are so strict: no electric points are allowed, and electric current should not be brought into such dangerous localities, not even by means of extension cables.

Quite apart from all this a tiny splash of water on the red-hot bulb makes it burst into a thousand fragments with a loud bang, scattering innumerable pointed glass splinters. This, incidentally, is also my own experience.

Paradoxically enough, you can work in the bathroom with high voltage without any fear if it is as safely protected as in the Braun Hobby electronic flash. Flashbulbs can, of course, also be used, since $22^1/2$ volts are completely harmless.

And now a few flash tips for the bathroom. It is very light – unless you are the owner of the "posh" type with black tiles. Thus you can make full use of your guide number, without modification. Indeed, this is perhaps the one place in the whole house where you may use half a stop smaller than the calculated value.

If possible, avoid pointing the flash at right angles to the tiles; otherwise you will discover the reflection of the flash in your transparency. Always point it at the wall at an oblique angle; it is easy to try it out beforehand with electronic flash, which costs nothing. Bathrooms are so light, and most of them also so narrow, that even a flash bounced from the ceiling will be effective. The considerably softer light will then be sufficient at f/4, since in any case we were able to photograph the splashing little devils at f/8 in direct flashlight. (You would, of course, get a terrible green cast if you made use of greentiled walls for your indirect flash light. Here, only direct flash light should be used.)

Here is a tip which may lead you to the crowning achievement of all your children's pictures. When one of your progeny is having fun under the shower, you first turn on the cosy warm tap. As soon as your camera is ready for action, one of the parents unkindly and suddenly turns it on cold, and the resulting cry is the signal to shoot. I can guarantee that your portrait will not lack expression.

Important Postscript

The amateur, who realises that the many things he can do with his flash means a considerable enlargement of his color photographic possibilities, will – in the long run – work more cheaply with an electronic flash unit than with expendable flash bulbs.

If you are the father – or mother – of small children, you will realise yourself that an ever-ready-to-flash Hobby F 60 unit can pay its way within as short a space as one year.

156

The more expensive, but also considerably more powerful Hobby Automatic with a capacity of 135 watt-seconds has made work with color film particularly attractive.

It is a well-known fact that reckoning with the guide number no longer holds good at distances below 5 feet. Even at 7 feet, the guide number calculation gives f/16. My practical experience has shown me that this stop can be retained if the subject is approached even more closely and absolutely nothing is gained by placing one or more flash-holders only a few inches away from it, even if you are forced to work at a very small camera distance through the use of close-focusing devices or the Dual Range focusing mount. In such cases it is preferable to separate the flash lamp from the camera, firing the flash from about 3 feet by means of a longer synchro-cable.

Even at f/16 very brightly colored subjects run the risk of being "over-flashed". Lenses which cannot be stopped down beyond f/16 do in fact call for the reduction of the flash power. The so warmly recommended use of two flashlamps from different directions has the same result as we all know; it also improves the quality of the lighting, so that f/16 with very bright objects, f/11–f/16 with darker objects will always produce good pictures with two flashlamps at 3 feet distance to the right and left.

I would again advise all flash fans not to adopt the confusing method of working with several guide numbers depending on whether they want to use their flash in their bathrooms or their coal cellars. The method of slightly increasing the stop according to the nature of the room or the absence of reflecting aids in the shape of walls and ceilings is considerably simpler and involves less risk. In the beginning at least, the recording of the exposure details i.e. flash distance and stop setting will be of great value. The result in color will readily show whether you are "on the right lines" or whether you will have to adjust your settings in future. A certain generosity in film consumption, say, 2–3 exposures on the same subject with slight alterations of the stop, will soon have paid for itself in terms of increased competence in your future work.

KUNGSGATAN, STOCKHOLM

December, midday, Stockholm.

The northern winter is hard, dark, and long, and the people are resigned to their climate as part of their lives.

During December and January, the days are never really light. When it rains or snows, the hour of noon passes more or less in a dull twilight.

What does not occur in our latitudes until 4 p.m. happens here at 2 p.m. during the same season. The first lights appear in the street scene.

Thus we see the reflections of the warm shopwindow lights on wet, cold pavements; and the people, who all seem to be anxious to be home and comfortable again; moreover, the snow-covered, parked cars, reflected as in a giant mirror in the wide windows: all this induced me to take this picture.

As camera viewpoint I chose a bridge leading across Stockholm's busy and popular Kungsgatan.

With the mainly vertical lines interrupted only intermittently by strong color effects, I wanted to emphasize the hustle and bustle of the passers-by. The two pictures on the following page show a similar expression, except that the lines there run more diagonally.

Leica, 50 mm. Summicron, f/2, $^1/_{15}$ second, December, 2 p.m.

158

THE FREEWAYS OF LOS ANGELES

This, too, is America, a restless, ever-moving country!
When the offices close, and the men drive to their far away homes,
or the women are homewards bound in their own cars from their
shopping expeditions in the super-market, there is the rush hour, the
famous hour between five and six p.m. Hell is loose in the streets, and
on the motor roads cars race, hiss, whirr, and flash past you; all this
– it is almost eerie – happens without hardly any sound! A mystical,
headlong, never-ending phantom procession.
At first I stood, my breath quite taken away, on one of the bridges,
built by the latest methods of technical perfection, which span the
arterial roads of Los Angeles. It was definitely too late for an instanta-
neous exposure; the exposure meter only reacted very sluggishly by
that time.
I, therefore, pressed my camera against the flat railings and exposed
– for the bottom picture – for about 2 seconds regardless of the cars
which, incidentally, did not travel at very great speeds. The deliberate
movement blur gives even more emphasis to the almost soundless
"swishing" noise.
I then hurried to the next bridge which gave me a view of the slowly
darkening horizon. Here, too, instantaneous exposures were no longer
possible. I, therefore, stopped my Summicron down as much as I could,
again pressed the Leica firmly against the railings and counted up to
60. Individual cars are no longer visible, instead, tail lights and head
lamps write long light tracks into the falling night. The minimum
stop permitted the long exposure time without at the same time over-
exposing the evening glow of the sky.

Top picture: Leica, 50 mm. Summicron, f/16, about 60 seconds, November, about
6 p.m.

Bottom picture: Leica, 50 mm. Summicron, f/2.8, about 2 seconds, November, about
6 p.m.

Really close-up

I have an unlimited admiration for those with unlimited patience. To them I raise my hat in reverence. Lest you get the wrong idea, I do not mean those who on an icy winter's day wait for hours getting cold feet, hands, and noses, looking skywards and praying for a tiny ray of sunlight. No, my admiration goes out to those amateurs who are able to work for hours and days for a single exposure. At times their reward is indeed only one, but then a really great, picture!

Walter Wissenbach is one of those patient souls I am talking about. His pictures of bats on the wing are photographic gems. Or those close-up views of freshly-hatched birds, being fed by their parents with flies and worms – all that can be seen of the tiny fledglings are their expectantly gaping, pink-lined yellow beaks. Or bees, whose whirring wings cannot even be recorded sharply by the $1/1000$ second of the electronic flash, sniffing at a flower – almost all of us know such pictures – and cannot help admiring them. I believe that only very few others have succeeded in taking such subjects.

Far be it from me to belittle the achievements of these patient masters of the camera, but I would say that close-up pictures up to the region of extreme macrophotography (i. e. objects appearing larger on the film than their natural size) are not quite as difficult to produce as it would seem. Detailed knowledge of the habits of wild animals and insects and, above all, patience are, of course, two important requirements. The third condition is purely technical – it can be bought in a shop. You must be able to extend your lens far out in front of your camera, whether by means of a specially long focusing mount, intermediate rings, near-focusing devices, bellows extensions, or the like.

A question of fractions of an inch

Close-up photographs are, of course, possible with supplementary front lenses, so that even amateurs owning cameras without interchangeable lenses can pursue this intriguing subject to some extent.

It is best to be able to judge the picture on a ground-glass screen, because the depth-of-field zone shrinks to a minimum in close-up pictures. After all, here we deal no longer with yards and feet, but with inches and fractions of inches. To return to our example of the bee in the flower, it is already quite a feat to get the bee and the rim of the flower alone completely inside the depth-of-field zone if you work at almost double the extension of your lens. At the extremely small stop of f/16, at a 1:1 reproduction ratio (and with a 135 mm. lens) the depth-of-field zone measures less than one tenth of an inch! You will therefore have to be quite satisfied if the bee is kind enough not to protude its abdomen into the picture, but offers a side view, nicely in one plane!

Increased exposure times

If you are interested in the extremely fascinating photography of close-up subjects, you would be well advised to study the very detailed description of the Leitz bellows unit. Here you will readily see that pictures closer than 3 feet invariably demand a longer distance between lens and film plane, that is extra lens extension. Quite apart from the rapid decrease of the depth of field in spite of our progressive stopping down, the exposure time becomes longer, too. It makes a noticeable difference whether we take pictures with a tele-lens at infinity or at 3 feet. Indeed, as I have already mentioned, we must open up by about half a stop at such close distances. However, the further the lens is moved from the film, the longer we must expose, even though the stop is unchanged. If we take photographs at same-size reproduction, the lens speed decreases to a quarter of its normal value, hence we must expose four times as long as our meter readings indicate.

However, I do not wish to fill this book with tables. They are obtainable without difficulty from your photo dealer, as they are part of all leaflets on close-up focusing devices.

It will be no surprise that hand-held exposures with these small stops and prolonged exposure times are impossible, no matter how good the lighting conditions. If ever there is a case for a tripod, this is it!

The ideal – electronic flash

Electronic flash, too, is a wonderful supplementary aid. Close-up views in sunlight, which, stopped down to f/11 and f/16, demand 1/25 second and longer in spite of increased film speeds can then be exposed at at least $^1/_{50}$ second. The electronic flash assumes the role of main light source, while the sun, which we can, if necessary, dispense with, becomes the fill-in light.

Walter Wissenbach's pictures of small and very small animals have almost invariably been possible only with the aid of electronic flash. His "sitters", in any case, do not normally nest in open, sunny places. On sites to be reached only with difficulty, hidden in the depths of undergrowth of shrubs and trees, he arranges his Leica and flash unit and takes up position himself with a yard-long cable release, so that the shy animals do not sense any danger.

Still life first

The close-up subjects that I take and which I think every beginner could master are situated not so much in the deep undergrowth of inaccessible forests, but in our immediate surroundings, about the house and in the garden. Anything you think might make an attractive close-up photograph you can obviously take in color, too. For example, a polished copper bowl filled with flowers, the geranium pot on the window sill, the tulips in the front garden, luminous in back light, as well as the little pansies.

Flower pieces indoors are not a difficult subject, they move less than blossoms and flowers outdoors; for even when the air appears to be

absolutely still, there is always some very slight movement about. Even a cloud obscuring the sun causes a momentary slight "shivering" of the plants. We notice it clearly when we observe the image on the ground-glass screen.

I should therefore advise you to take your first close-up photographs indoors. Incident daylight near the window as main light source and a white reflector, sheet, or paper, or even a mirror serve to soften the heavy shadows. Such experiments can give you much pleasure, and your best friend is the tripod.

Naturally, you could also make hand-held exposures under very good lighting conditions. However, the tripod also has a task other than the prevention of camera-shake: since the observation of the field of view is based on fractions of an inch the camera must, if possible, keep to the intended picture field. A tripod leaves your hands free to manipulate your subject at will and to experiment with your reflecting aids. Moreover, you will soon find out for yourself that you will need more depth of field.

Neutralizing the background

But how about outdoors? Of course, larger objects such as the sunflower are easy, due to their tall growth. All we have to do is to bend down and the brilliant bloom will be pictured clearly against the sky; and we are doubly fortunate that the two complementary colors, blue and yellow, contrast so very well.

On the other hand, daisies, dandelions, and the like usually grow in luscious meadows in the immediate neighbourhood of sorrel, sage, and other intruders we do not wish to include in our picture.

Take a piece of cardboard, a small cloth (of one color, dark, and neutral, if possible), and let someone hold it about 6 inches behind your flower "model". For once it does not matter that all the other grass and plants are pressed down, if you focus your camera accurately. Here, too, ground-glass screen control by means of the Visoflex will prove particularly useful.

Now the depth of field should not be so great as to include the cardboard, too. However, the distance of 6 inches is large enough, so that it cannot be recognized as cardboard any more. Very ingenious people make doubly sure of absolute unsharpness by having the cardboard moved to and fro a little during longer exposure times. (An assistant is almost indispensable here, but we must be careful not to cause any draught!)

Dark cardboard or sheets are better as neutralizing background than light, not to mention white material, indoors as well as outdoors. We must always bear the color reflections in mind; on a green meadow, a color reflection is bound to occur on a white surface. This again

165

leads to the grumble: – you see, green cast! Grey, and, above all, black backgrounds absorb colors and are therefore immune to color cast.

On every one of these occasions you will improve your close-up photographs by using supplementary flash. The heavy shadows will acquire nice detail, and a picture, taken perhaps without sun, will appear to all the world as if it had shone from a cloudless sky.

Photography of objects closer than 3 feet is the perfect therapy for nervous and worn-out people whom sudden relaxation and inactivity tends to make even more nervous. Photography ought to be prescribed for such people, it acts like a tonic, except that this remedy is a stimulant rather than a tranquillizer.

All kinds of copying

Copying, of course, also belongs to the category of close-up photography, except that it offers a great advantage compared with breezy little flowers and humming bees: the objects have little depth, most of them are very flat, and, of course, little trouble arises regarding depth of field.

I am often asked how paintings can be taken as faithfully as possible. One thing is certain: it is most difficult to do it in their normal surroundings on the wall. In our homes, the illumination is not only frequently affected by colored curtains or wallpaper, there are also light reflections which have to be avoided; museums are mostly too dark, or photography is prohibited there.

The experts are not agreed whether it is better to copy these subjects in direct sunlight or in dull weather. My advice is neither-nor, although I would be inclined to favour direct sunlight. If natural light is to be used at all, hazy sunlight seems to me to be the most suitable. However, we never "know" our light exactly and will always be a little "at sea" with every fresh exposure.

In order to be quite sure, I therefore prefer the artificial sunlight from my Braun Hobby, and the assistance of natural daylight will create no difficulties at all.

Avoid reflections

First of all we must see to it that our original, whether it is an oil painting or water color under glass, is completely free from reflections. To take pictures from their frames in order to photograph them without glass is easier said than done. Most of them are stuck down on the back firmly enough to last a lifetime, so that we cannot persuade ourselves to do it. Reframing them, too, is too cumbersome. It is thus preferable to experiment with pictures under glass until, viewed exactly from the camera position, they are free from reflections. This is possible by turning them slightly this way or that, and especially by tilting them forward a little. If the whole set-up is taken by flash, a helper carefully tilting the frame forward can hold the picture even during the exposure.

At any rate, illumination with two flashes is the safest method. We must take care that the lighting is uniform obliquely from the left and right. If we arrange the lamps at 45° to the plane of the picture we will avoid disturbing reflections. A flash directly behind the camera is bound to produce a large splash of light on originals prone to reflections. Here, too, the extension flash, with a splitting-up of the flashlight between left and right, proves to be the most elegant and reliable solution.

If we only have one flash reflector, the whole thing is postponed until

167

the evening or the room is blacked out to exclude any stray light. A weak bulb in the ceiling allows us sufficient light to see in. We then set our camera at "T", opening the shutter. We walk from left to right, firing the two flashes, which otherwise would have gone off simultaneously, in succession. Only we must bear in mind here that two successively fired electronic flashes yield more light than two flash heads fired together.

Uniform lighting distance with different originals

If you want to copy pictures, drawings, and other colored originals frequently, you can work with a standard illumination. If both flash lamps always give their light from about 5 to 7 feet distance, it is immaterial whether they illuminate a large picture or a small one. The photograph can be taken independently from the flash at camera distances of 10 feet or 3 feet. The required stop is accurately known, and all that has to be taken care of is that the original should fill the entire picture area, if possible.

If you take color transparencies, this cannot always be achieved, since not every picture accurately corresponds to the film size. Therefore a dark, neutral support should be chosen, or the transparency should be masked.

Never copy your originals by flash in rooms with colored walls. You should make detailed notes about lighting distance and stop numbers. This will in time give you such confidence that you will soon need only one color film for 36 copies – you will be one hundred per cent successful!

Color Negative Film for Colored Originals

For reproductions of paintings, drawings etc. I like to take color negative film. After all, in most cases color paper prints are needed rather than slides, and since the color reproduction must approach the original very closely, it will in certain conditions be essential to show the original to the color technician for correct filter assessment.

The negative film offers the advantage that the reproduction can be taken in daylight, with flash, as well as in artificial light. The advantage of photoflood lamps consists in a stricter control of the lighting and the possibility of avoiding reflections. But we must beware of mixed lighting and eliminate daylight as much as possible when working with artificial light.

When the Sun Sets

Gabriele R.   Baden near Zurich 5/4/1957.

D e a r   M r .   B e n s e r ,

A few months ago you gave us so much pleasure with your
lecture at Zurich, that not only did we buy a Leica a few
days later, but also started with color film right away.
If you want to know what caught our particular fancy, it
was your sunset pictures, because from our home here we
can see a marvelous sunset almost every day. So we tried
immediately to do as well as you. But our results were
deplorable. They were indeed so bad, that we enclose them
with our letter to enable you to put us on the right
track. (You need not return them, the waste-paper basket
is the only place for these transparencies.)
The pictures, then, are far too pale, and the sun only
looks like a tiny dot. Moreover, yellow splashes of light
appear in the foreground on all pictures, so that we
suspected a fault in the camera. But friends of ours
think that they are due to internal reflections in the
lens. Does this always happen, and how can we avoid it?
When will you come to Zurich again? We learned much last
time, but not enough, or else we would not have to write
to you now. Yours sincerely,   N. N.
P. S. We also have a good exposure meter. However, without doubt it has given the wrong reading of the sunset:
1/2 second at f/5.6. Isn't this far too much?

Walther Benser   Düsseldorf, 19th April, 1957

D e a r   M a d a m ,

Here is my reply. Yes, your transparencies are without
exception greatly over-exposed, but your exposure meter
is not at fault! For your exposure measurement – using
the so-called direct reading method – gives you, as it
were, a cross-section of the brightness of the measured
object. Thus, in your case it covered a part which was
unimportant to the picture – your garden and a vast por-
tion of the more or less silhouette-like landscape. The

sinking sun and the evening sky, then, contributed at
best only 50 per cent to your measurement.
I believe it is invariably better with such pictures to
rely on one's own or someone else's experience. This, at
any rate, says that in such instances the average exposure time ranges between f/5.6 and f/8 and 1/25 second.
I would even be inclined to cut down on the exposure
further still, depending on the sun's position, the
brilliance of the background (lake, or river), because
nothing could be worse here than a generous exposure.
And now a word about the reflections in the foreground
(you have the sun not once, but as many as three times
in your picture). This is a phenomenon which is unavoidable so long as the sun still dazzles as much as it
has done on your pictures. You ought to have waited a few
more minutes until it had sunk a little lower, when the
dazzle would have decreased very rapidly; you find again
and again that shortly before sunset you can look
straight into the fire-ball even without sun-glasses and
without squinting. This is the moment when you can take
your photographs without fear of disturbing reflections!
Now it is not always possible to get a good picture of
the sun at the very last moment. This depends a great
deal on the weather. Sometimes you will find that a layer
of haze above the horizon swallows up and obscures the
sun. Let us maintain, then, that the correct moment for
our exposure has arrived whenever we are able to look
into the sun. There are even hazy or misty days, on which
one can photograph straight into the sun even at mid-day
without the risk of reflections. If you insist on taking
your sunset pictures from your balcony, please await the
right moment patiently next time. However, you must
remember that the landscape in the foreground will only
show up as a dark shape, that is, as a silhouette. But as
your foreground does not appear to be particularly
interesting — I do not, by any means, wish to imply that
the view from your house is anything but lovely — it
would be preferable to tilt the camera a little upwards
and to displace the foreground to the bottom margin of
your picture, where it will only show as a dark fringe.
Have you bought a tripod yet? If not you can use your
balcony as camera support by pushing a slightly wedge-
shaped piece of wood under your Leica. This will guard
you fairly well against camera-shake, because a hand-held
1/25 second is a little risky. May I give you yet another

tip? You know Lake Zug, don't you? The lake promenade
directly leading out of Zug is in my opinion a downright
classical spot for sunsets. The golden light track of the
setting sun will lead right up to your feet if you go
close enough to the water's edge. And if my memory serves
me right you can even take weeping willows into your
foreground, and a few rowing boats as silhouettes. A few
years ago I passed the place and saw at once what I could
have photographed. However, a lecture at Lucerne made any
break in my journey impossible.

Lastly, sooner or later you will make up your mind to
acquire a longer focal length lens. Not only because it
enables you to pull in your selected picture areas far
more effectively. Naturally, the sun, too, will appear
larger, and the 90 mm. Elmar turns the tiny dot into a
sizeable blob. The picture out of my lecture series you
admired so much was taken with the 135 mm. Hektor, which
reproduces the sun at almost three times the size of the
"normal" picture. Hence the striking effect! If I am not
mistaken, I even mentioned the exposure data at the time
(25 ASA) 1/50 second at f/4.5. You see, it must be far
shorter than you tried yourself.

I will be very pleased if I have helped you a little with
these tips.

How about bringing along your new sunsets and showing
them to me at my next lecture? Hope to see you at the
"Kaufleuten".

When the Moon Rises

Many amateurs will find it unlikely that one can really take color photographs by moonlight. As a matter of fact, they are so successful that at excessively long exposure times photographs are obtained which are almost undistinguishable from those taken in hazy sunlight. However, such an experiment could not be our aim. Instead of "collecting" moonlight for 20 minutes from a tripod it is easier and quicker to obtain a color picture in daylight at $1/100$ second, and it will be more brilliant into the bargain!

On the other hand, things begin to become interesting when the color film only receives sufficient moonlight for the twilight impression to be preserved, and the moonlight atmosphere of the picture is recognized at first sight.

To begin with, I would distinguish between two basically different kinds of moon pictures. Firstly those in which the moon itself can be seen, and secondly where it stands behind or above us in order to illuminate the subject. And you will even be told in this chapter how to "plant" the moon where it has never been.

Only one $1/500.000$ part of the sunlight

Moonlight is reflected sunlight, more precisely $1/500.000$ of the sun's brightness. Purely from an arithmetical point of view, three to five minutes at f/4 would not by a long stretch represent a sufficient exposure. However, it is a fact that long after sunset there is still twilight about, which is no longer registered by our eye. It helps to reduce the exposure considerably. The caption of the moonlight picture of Mürren in the Bernese Oberland gives you the description of a photograph by moonlight. Obviously, the picture is entirely dependent on the lit-up little windows for its effect. The yellow, given undue emphasis by the daylight color film, contrasts, according to my taste, particularly pleasingly with the cooler general blue of the snow-covered landscape. It is also the be-all and end-all of all similar subjects to take lighted windows into the picture, because they emphasize the night atmosphere and leave no doubt about the subject.

Another piece of incontrovertible, though pictorially not so effective evidence of a night picture are the stars. Depending on their brightness they form short luminous tracks in the sky during the minutes of our exposure.

Full moon is best

Obviously, the best illumination is available on a night with a full moon. A night before or after full moon will also be satisfactory. However, when the moon is clearly waxing or waning, the exposure times will increase considerably. Full moon does not, as we should expect, reflect twice as much, but fully seven times as much light as the moon at the first or last quarter, because during full moon the sun's rays fall fairly perpendicularly on the surface of the moon visible to us, while during half-moon they reach it at an oblique angle, so that the high lunar mountains cast shadows on a large part of our satellite.

It is better not to rely on what you think you see, or on the romantic exclamations of your girl- (or boy-) friend as to whether or not the moon is full. The calendar is far more trustworthy.

Nor, unfortunately, can we always rely on the weather. If you intend climbing a certain peak on February 14th at full moon in order to take the Moonlight Picture of Your Life at four minutes' exposure time, you may be frustrated on that very day by rain or snow, and photography is completely out of the question. Overcast sky would not be so bad, because the light from the moon still illuminates the landscape sufficiently through high, perhaps a little broken-up cloud.

Let me tell you of my friend Roland Bühler, postmaster at Mürren, Switzerland, and in his spare time a photo fanatic with a kind of obsession which makes him undergo any hardships in order to obtain pictures. He has been trying for more than two years now to achieve the ideal moonlight photograph. He even has the good luck to live only a few hundred yards from the most outstanding vantage point of the whole mountain world.

With a bit of luck there is continuous snow from December to April at this famous winter resort; the chalets, too, are covered by quaint snow caps, so typical of a mountain village during the winter. Thus, the moonlight idyll with Eiger, Mönch, and Jungfrau in the background will only occur about five times a year. However, poor old Roland has been trying desperately for two years to get a decent picture, and for two years it simply could not be done, because either fog or snow during full moon made photography impossible.

Finally, during April of the second year, everything seemed to be set fair. However, the full moon – scheduled to rise at 8 p.m. according to the calendar – happened to dawdle so much on its long path behind the high mountain range that it did not appear from behind Eiger until after 9 o'clock. It took a further two hours to detach itself from Eiger and to climb into the sky so that it would not look like a fat, white line in the picture. But during this time of waiting one light after the other went out in the village, except for a few lighted windows of some late hotel guest, who unfortunately lived far too much in the background.

It would, of course, be useless to include the moon in the picture and to expose for six minutes. In as short a time as two minutes the moon travels through the distance of its own diameter, and instead of the beautiful, large, golden yellow disc, the photograph would show a not-so-beautiful golden yellow cucumber. Furthermore, the light intensity of *back-lighting* light from the moon – there is such a thing, too, you know – is too weak. (How quickly the moon moves on its course we can discover with the naked eye when it emerges from behind a mountain ridge.)

In addition, to take a "portrait" of the moon alone at a short exposure is also rather pointless. Since it betrays movement after a minimum exposure time of 15 seconds showing a bulge in the direction of its movement, you may well succeed in a picture of the moon, but the intriguing contours of the beautiful nocturnal snowscape will not come out at all.

Moon at dusk

Only one, relatively rare, opportunity exists of recording moon and landscape at the same time and at sufficiently short exposure times: if the moon rises at dusk, shining within the angle of view of your camera, a few thumbs' breadths above the horizon. This will give us lighting from the back from a sky (aurora) so bright that we can photograph the landscape bathed in moonlight – perhaps a lake with lit-up houses along its shore – at exposure times from 5 to 15 seconds. I found that the favorable conditions – dusk and rising moon – occur during November and December.

However, who guarantees us reliably a brightly-reflecting blanket of snow and broken-up cloud during this part of the year? And on the following evening it no longer works out! (Consulting your calendar you will notice that the moon rises three-quarters of an hour later every day!)

Trick photographs with the genuine moon

I thought out a picture (just for fun) which, although it involves a little cheating, is still possible with the genuine moon and a genuine landscape. This, then, is my imaginary picture:

On an ideal full moon night I stand in front of an ideal brightly-reflecting subject, with the moon high in the sky behind me. Whether the subject is a snowcovered village in the montains or white huts of an Arab town is immaterial, as long as light shines from the windows, and the houses are close enough. The exposure time is known; f/4 (and, of course, from the tripod – hand-held pictures are out of the question!) and about 3 minutes' exposure. (This is the correct time for an 50 ASA film. You will need about double the exposure time for less sensitive color films. Incidentally, a few minutes more do not make a great deal of difference here.)

Now at the end of the exposure the shutter is not closed. Instead, I put the lens cap or my hand over my camera lens, when I can turn the camera on its tripod through an angle of 180° without any trouble; I arrange the moon through the viewfinder or on the ground-glass screen precisely on the spot I had "left empty" for it previously above the Arab huts or the mountain village.

The lens cap is removed, I count two leisurely seconds, and the full moon is safely in the picture by means of a double exposure trick! By the way, the full moon will be on the film even at $1/10$ second, but over-exposure does no harm at all in this case. Hardly anyone will notice the forgery afterwards, though they could prove it by means of the shadows cast in the wrong direction.

If, in addition, you are the owner of a long focal length lens, or even a fat, long tele-lens, you will be able to approach your subject with added ingenuity; you can photograph the buildings with a shorter focal length lens and replace this (at some speed, since the shutter must remain open) by a longer focal length lens (covered by the lens cap!). Now the camera is turned round, and the moon arranged in the appropriate position. Finally, another two seconds' exposure for the moon – which, due to the longer focal length lens with which it was taken, will be reproduced at a convincing size. The whole trick should be patiently repeated several times.

Collecting light effects by stopping down

And finally a few short words about f/4 which I mentioned in connection with my moonlight pictures. Why not, say, f/5.6 or even f/8? (Let me tell you about the subject "sharpness through smaller stops" in the next chapter.) Back to our moonlight in bitter winter cold, I repeat, cold!! This first and foremost was the determining factor for my choice of f/4. A smaller stop, such as f/5.6, will perhaps increase to its maximum the general sharpness of the wide-angle lens used. Here, however, it was my chief concern not to have to expose for prolonged periods, because f/5.6 demands twice, f/8 four times the exposure time of f/4, that is twelve minutes. And as on such occasions

I am never content with one picture only, it would take me too long to get them all finished (the six minutes of the picture of Mürren seemed like eternity to me. That was with 15° DIN Agfacolor film).

Why, then, did I not shorten this cold time of waiting even further by opening up my stop yet more? Assuming I would have had a sufficient angle of view with the standard focal length lens and used its maximum aperture of f/2. Obviously, this would have been possible, but it would have represented the other extreme; I would have found the exposure time of about one minute insufficient on account of the lit-up windows in the village.

You see, down in the village, the people are sitting down to their supper, turning the lights on in their dining rooms, switching them off in their kitchens. Here a blind is shut, there another one is opened. A shop door opens for a second ... yet another dot of light in my picture, and so on and so forth. The longer we can expose, the more lights will therefore be collected in the photograph.

In the mad picture on p. 161 with its hundreds of motor cars on the Los Angeles freeways, light snakes of headlamps and tail lights writhe through the picture right to the horizon. These "light spaghetti" I owe to the deliberately prolonged exposure with the minimum stop!

Don't be Scared of Large Stops!

We sometimes are told "pinsharp pictures can only be obtained with f/8 and smaller stops". People who hold this opinion photograph too little and read too much.

"Rubbish" is the only correct, if rude reply to them. Naturally, camera lenses vary in their quality. But let us consider the class of the Leica lenses sparkling in the bluish sheen of their coated surfaces. If we have such first-class, and therefore expensive, lenses in our camera, there is no harm in opening up our stops as far to the left as they will go, operating, as it were, at full throttle. We focus for maximum sharpness with the coupled rangefinder, when we can expose, even under poor lighting conditions, $^1/_{50}$ or $^1/_{60}$ second respectively at f/2, out of hand.

We could repeat the exposure for comparison purposes at f/4 and $^1/_{10}$ second – which, as we know, amounts to the same in practice. However, if the second exposure is also hand-held, I would bet that the first picture will be sharper!

Which brings us to the basic purpose of the large stop. The high speed of a lens is, above all, an insurance against the dangers of camera-shake and subject movement under unfavourable light conditions.

By the way, did you know that an f/2 lens at its maximum aperture is less susceptible to so-called internal reflection (ghost images of the iris diaphragm) than when it is stopped down?

Try to photograph into a bright searchlight or headlamp at full aperture. You could do it in the circus or on the road at night. Unless you stop down, you will see these ghost images only very rarely, if at all.

Let me return once more to the rumour that smaller stops result in better image sharpness. Perhaps this is due to a confusion of depth of field with general resolution. We all know that great depth of field affects the picture from foreground to background in its entire depth. On the other hand, the sharpness of the lens is tested in the plane on which it is focused from one picture corner to the other. In this connection, we are naturally also interested in the color reproduction. If the corners of the picture become darker we talk about "vignetting".

This can be rather unpleasant if a perfectly exposed landscape picture shows a fall-off in brightness towards all four corners, particularly in the sky. I know these regrettable effects – but only from pictures taken by others, never from my own (unless I had used too long a lens hood)!

How much shall – or can – we stop down?

Occasionally we read or hear that although the performance of a lens improves with stopping down, it deteriorates again after having reached its optimum at a certain stop.

This is correct, but always it depends on the type of lens. In addition, in order to prove this ascending and descending sharpness curve, very complicated and critical test exposures are necessary. In practice you can safely stop Leica lenses down to f/16 if the depth of field requires it. You will be unable to detect any loss of sharpness due to this stopping down.

Remains the question to be answered at which stop the maximum of general sharpness is reached. According to the type of lens the maximum sharpness generally lies between f/4 and f/8. My statement that very intricate tests of the famous Summicron lens have shown this maximum to lie at f/4 will, I am sure, amaze you, because for a fast lens this is an astonishingly early peak. You will hardly be in a position of checking this, because the transition from the surprisingly good sharpness already present at full aperture to the still greater sharpness at f/4 is almost imperceptible. It cannot be detected even with a strong magnifying glass.

My standard: f/5.6 or f/8

Nevertheless, this value should not be adopted as the standard stop, although the resulting short exposure time is in many cases a great help. On the other hand, the depth of field is not sufficient with near subjects, so that for all normal exposure subjects f/5.6 or f/8 should be accepted as the most favorable stop.

Wide-angle lenses generally reach their optimum performance only later apart from the pronounced tendency inherent in the nature of short focal lengths towards vignetting. This is less evident in black-and-white than in color photographs, because here a sky darkening towards the corners clearly shows up the disadvantages of lenses prone to vignetting.

179

A wide-angle lens can be used at full aperture without difficulty whenever the camera is not pointed at an open landscape, but is used for snapshots of all kinds. The astonishingly fast 35 mm. Summicron f/2 can therefore be opened up fully without trouble if poor lighting conditions make it necessary. With satisfactory light we stop in any case down to medium apertures of say f/5.6 or f/8, so that landscape subjects are not exposed to the risk of vignetting.

In the case of the super-wide angle, the 21 mm. Angulon, though, a stopping down to f/8, or better still, f/11, is recommended for subjects with uniform color areas, particularly sky.

It must be mentioned in passing that in the field of fast and ultra-fast lenses everything is still in a state of flux. Only a few years ago it was thought absolutely impossible to compute efficient lenses of short focal lengths at such large apertures. New types of glass and the advent of electronic computers, however, led the way to astonishing results.

Which Standard Lens should be Bought?

Every amateur wishing to start color photography with a good camera comes up against the question: – What camera, what lens, what speed?

As an inveterate Leica man I am biased about the camera, in the case of the lens my answer is this: – If you can at all afford it, settle for a fast one, because the progress in computing optics has assured already quite outstanding performance at full apertures.

This has not always been the case. When f/3.5 lenses were the standard, every increase in speed had to be paid for with inferior picture quality. These faster lenses had to be stopped down considerably in order to equal roughly the performance of the f/3.5 lenses. Some people to whom lens speed was essential had several lenses of the same focal length. Whenever they could do without maximum speed they quickly fell back on their f/3.5 lens.

Today you need no longer duplicate your standard lens, you should merely consider whether you need high lens speed at all rather than that of a slower standard lens, when you could buy, with the money saved, a second lens of a different focal length.

Another way already hinted at would be the purchase of a fast 35 mm. wide-angle as the first lens, followed by the addition of a 90 mm. long-distance lens.

180

Night in the Big City

The most favorable time for exposures begins at lighting-up time, when the shops switch their window lights on, and the street lamps are turned on. All this happens with daylight still very much in evidence.

This daylight is a wonderful help. You can, and even should, continue using daylight color film. I show you a typical example in the picture of Kungsgatan, Stockholm, on p. 143.

The slowly fading daylight also helps us to avoid the large "black holes", because at night hardly any lit-up windows show in the upper floors of the many office blocks in the centre of a large city. Every here and there such a lonely square can be found in the dark, but the outline of the building is almost lost. Generally, office work ceases at 5 or 6 p.m., and afterwards such buildings no longer offer much to the camera.

December is the most favorable month

The wonderful time for night pictures occurs during December afternoons and also includes the first half of January. December, however, is best, because the Christmas season, with its increasing commercialization, offers veritable cascades of light. Not enough that individual neon light advertising tries to outdo its neighbours; endless rows of lamps cover the shopping streets like luminous chains. In addition, it often rains during these weeks, so that the flood of light is intensified by reflection in the wet asphalt.

But the most important point is this: Dusk begins before 5 p.m., while work is still going on in the offices. Thousands of brightly lit windows high up to the top floors illuminate the city, everything being spanned by the evening sky slowly changing into a deeper blue. At this hour we can without fear expose color daylight film (50 ASA) at f/2.8 and $1/25$ or $1/30$ second in brightly lit streets. Naturally, one can ring the changes here either by opening the lens fully or even stopping down a little. The decisive point here is the number of light sources and whether we have wet asphalt to reflect them or not. Partial overexposures no longer play their dreaded role under these conditions.

The pictures become generally brighter, perhaps here and there a highlight becomes burnt out, but it disappears among the hundreds of tiny light spots and dots. In contrast with the general demand for large and quiet color areas, in the city at night there is no harm in accepting the multitude of scintillating lights in their thousands of variations. The more the waning daylight pulls the picture together by revealing the buildings the better.

Exposure times also depend on exposure distances

My tip of the short hand-held exposure (^{1}/$_{25}$ second at f/2.8) is only valid if we stand in the centre of activities. Reflections and light therefore must, so to speak, start right at our feet. As soon as we photograph a general view of far-away light points, we need a considerably increased exposure time; we shall arrive at several seconds when it will be extremely difficult to give reliable information without the risk of misleading you.

Since ^{1}/$_{25}$ or ^{1}/$_{30}$ second already represent the limit of possible instantaneous exposures, we shall quite frequently have to employ long "instantaneous" – or to be more honest – short "time" exposures, which really start at ^{1}/$_{10}$ second. Now a little camera-shake at ^{1}/$_{10}$ or ^{1}/$_{15}$ second is not really a calamity, and during projection we will be able to get away with it. Be that as it may, sharp pictures, which we most obviously must take from a tripod or a tripod substitute are better. In town we shall always find a firm support for our camera somewhere, such as a lamp-post which can serve us as a camera prop. For vertical pictures, we press the camera against it with its base plate. For horizontal pictures we can place it on rings, ornaments, or other protruding features making it possible to expose for the short times between ^{1}/$_{10}$ and 1 second without camera-shake.

Universal table-top tripod

But these are only makeshift measures. A tripod is better. Here, too, we have several variations to choose from. The possibilities of the table-top tripod are far too little realized. It had to be given a name somehow, although its use is by no means restricted to the top of a table. It will work admirably when pressed against a vertical wall. However, such a table-top tripod is a somewhat primitive affair without a ball-and-socket head which alone will enable us to adjust our

182

camera at a moment's no-
tice for vertical and horizontal exposures. If we
want to leave our large
tripod at home, we simply
unscrew our ball-and-socket head from it, trans-
ferring it to our table-top
tripod.

Once in New York I
wanted to take twilight
pictures from the platform
of the Rockefeller Build-
ing where the use of tri-
pods is prohibited. I used
the table-top tripod as a
perfect substitute, pushing
it far to the front on the
broad parapet, offering
my Leica a view of the
yawning depths below. In
this way, an exposure of
6 secs. presented no dif-
ficulty.

At night – artificial light color film

Whether you take whole streets or a solitary sausage vendor at the
Christmas Fair, I admit that all night exposures on daylight color
film will show a strong yellow bias. This contradicts our memory
which tells us that the lights and lamps were white. This is quite
understandable, since we offer lights with color temperatures ranging mainly between 2.600° and 3.600° K. to a film expecting far
higher color temperatures. Only the daylight still playing its part
during dusk compensates, with its saturated blue-grey, the somewhat
excessive yellow color of the artificial illumination.

But what happens when the night sky stands black above the city,
and the daylight has completely vanished? In order to make it easy
for the amateur, the advice generally offered is to continue using daylight color film, particularly since in practice it has been found that

183

the insertion of a special artificial light color film is cumbersome. After all, we hardly ever expect to shoot 20 or 36 artificial light subjects in a single evening, and the film therefore remains in the camera. Three days later, we have forgotten all about it and merrily continue using artificial color film in bright daylight; the result – ice-blue pictures – is horrible!

The color temperature of the daylight film could also be adjusted for artificial light by the use of an appropriate conversion filter (B 6 and one stop larger). However, who goes to the trouble of doing that? One thing, though, is certain; night photographs in the city have truer colors and also more brilliance if taken on artificial light film!

Circus, music hall, and theater

It is very difficult to take photographs in the theater, primarily because it is not usually allowed. And this is as it should be, for would it not also irritate you, as a member of the audience, if someone in your neighborhood raised his camera to his eye every few minutes, clicking the shutter? It is every bit as disturbing as people pulling sweets from rustling cellophane bags during the performance.

Also, it is not very rewarding to take photographs from a front row seat if we can move neither to the left nor to the right. Whether or not

we like it, we shall always have more or less the whole scene in our picture. If it is brightly lit, and the actors do not gesticulate too wildly, well-exposed color pictures of sufficient sharpness are possible at the maximum aperture of f/2 and with a gentle release of the shutter at $^1/_{10}$ to $^1/_{15}$ second. If ever the artificial color film offers an advantage over its daylight brother, it is here.

Better pictures than from the front rows can be obtained from the side part of the balcony. If necessary, even without the permission of the management. I chance it every now and again, propping my camera secretly on the edge of the balcony. If it is not too softly upholstered, it forms a useful substitute for a tripod. The most wonderful lens, even for choosing parts from the scene, is a longer focal length with a large aperture.

The later Leica models no longer emit an audible "click". This has now become so subdued that I cannot find an appropriate word for it. "Click" sounds too loud. Perhaps you will accept "muffled click" or "butter-soft click"! Nevertheless there are moments in the theater where you could literally hear a pin drop; when, of course, one can also hear your Leica. People become annoyed, turn round, all their illusions are destroyed. It is difficult to take photographs in the theater . . . but it is easier at variety shows and easier still in the circus. For such occasions I always take my Summarit along because its f/1.5 aperture is twice as large as the Summicron's f/2.

Know your program

The most important condition for successful theater, circus, and variety show photography is knowledge of the performance or the program and to have information about the sequence of scenes and climaxes.

Otherwise you will sometimes use up your entire film for the somewhat tedious elephants' number and find afterwards with consternation that the polar bears on bicycles were far more amusing and, in addition, better lit.

You should therefore watch the entire program beforehand, noting its photographic climaxes! Perhaps you will on this occasion also find out which seat will afford you the best photographic views on your next visit.

In the circus I permit myself the luxury of a box, taking at the most only one companion with me. We try our charm on the lady at the cash desk to obtain a seat in the front row. I thus have only one stranger next to me to give me dirty looks for my camera antics, and do not run the risk of receiving accidental knocks from both sides.

Between ¹/₂ and ¹/₂₅ second

I take my tripod along but do not set it up, simply because there is no room for it. I only use it with its three legs closed, but somewhat extended, providing me with a rigid "unipod" which I can use sitting down for exposure times of ¹/₁₀ or ¹/₅ second, easily possible for not too fast-moving scenes.

The ushers in their fancy uniforms (from the rank of admiral upwards) mostly show understanding for photo enthusiasts, closing both eyes while you slink behind the stalls around the ring during the performance in order to find different viewpoints for your camera. You must not forget to climb up to the back row, from where you can take – perhaps with a wide-angle lens – the half circle of the audience together with the brilliantly lit circle of the arena. Even if from a rigid support you expose at ¹/₂ second then, certain unsharpnesses due to movement are not necessarily disturbing, because there will be atmosphere in the picture. Come on, have a go!

And remember: artificial light color film only!

Of course, one could also suggest using the Hobby flash from the stalls. Up to about 17 feet (and closer) you can do without the flood lights, employing your own light source. However, this calls for daylight color film! Although this will reproduce the background lit by the floodlights in a yellow color, I for one do not find this objectionable. But to use flash at the circus it is absolutely imperative that you have permission from the management and the performers themselves beforehand.

It is astonishing that even with generous exposures we do not obtain total failures as quickly as we would with subjects in daylight. Naturally, a brightly-illuminated scene – some spotlights are able to pick out one figure alone – is bound to result in falsified colors. However, if ring or stage are reasonably uniformly lit, the transparencies, although considerably lighter, will not be useless for this reason.

I once saw a stage color photograph in an American photographic magazine, shot from the top of the wings obliquely down on to the stage. A ballet, whose dancers gyrated in wide, billowing skirts in a waltz. In the centre, on tip-toe – the prima ballerina motionless in a dancing pose. The photographer had stopped down and exposed for a whole second without regard for the whirling dance of the other girls. The deliberate unsharpness of movement around the sharply-defined centre gave the photograph an attraction quite its own. Therefore, extreme sharpness is not always the most important factor.

Thunderstorm at night

Let me confess right away – I have not yet photographed a real flash of lighting. By this I mean lightning in the night sky, with many zigzags, just as a lightning flash should be.

Once, however, the great moment arrived, during our holidays (3 a.m. and apocalyptic fury outside). Again and again our bedroom was as light as day when the flashes writhed through the sky. I was immediately wide awake, jumped out of my bed and feverishly prepared my Leica and tripod. My wife protested desperately: one should never stand by an open window during a thunderstorm, this attracted lightning and was sheer suicide. While I opened the window undismayed, a lively dispute ensued about mortality rates of lightning strokes, old peasant lore (according to which oak trees should be avoided, but beeches sought as shelters against the storm) and other dubious advice for nocturnal travellers in need of protection.

Outside, the raging storm, behind me another one about to break – my attention thus divided unfortunately made me turn the iris of my Summicron down towards the right instead of opening it up towards the left. I wanted full aperture, instead

I stopped down to the minimum! And in the end I had such lovely flashes bang in the centre of the field of view of my camera which was patiently waiting on its tripod with, of course, its shutter open! Result: – 0.000 – dark, black night – or "Egyptian burial chamber before its discovery".

To take photographs of lightning flashes during the daytime would be tantamount to attempting to attack in a dark wood with a pin an enemy who, similarly armed with a pin, groped his way towards you from a far distance. The chances of the points of the pins meeting in the dark are about the same as those of capturing a flash with your camera during daytime. Because it has passed long before you really saw it. Perhaps you might note that lightning flashes should only be photographed at night, but with daylight color film, with the camera, with its shutter open, pointing in the direction of maximum lightning activity. By this method you can "collect" several flashes.

Taking Photographs Economically

A colour film has 20 or 36 exposures. The short 20 exposure length is designed for the benefit of those amateurs who do not use their cameras a great deal and do not want to wait too long for the film to be finished. The long, 36 exposure film is really more economical as it yields almost double the number of pictures although it is by no means twice as expensive. It ought to be possible to squeeze 37 out of it – but the instructions for its use give the well-founded advice to make blank exposures on the first 2–3 frames, because there is no guarantee that a little light might not steal on to the film through the cassette mouth during its insertion into the camera. You will see it yourself when you look at the beginning of your developed color film; often a brilliant red color can be seen along the first inch or two of the film starting from its cut end – evidence that the film was inserted in bright light.

Load your camera in the shade

And this is the reason for loading your camera at least in the shadow of your own body and never in direct sunlight! Better still, loading should take place in a shady room and best, of course, in the darkroom, where pre-fogging is completely avoided, and the film can be exposed safely after one or two blank exposures only. Thus you may get 37 pictures out of your 36 exposure cassette.

A glance at the film counter of the camera shows when 36 pictures have been exposed. Some people do not notice this and turn the film on with determination. At last the cassette gives in to the force applied, and the films is torn from the spool. Some continue merrily taking their pictures, pleased perhaps at the thought that the film manufacturers have wound a few more inches of film on to the spool to show their generosity. But at picture No. 45 at the latest, things begin to look alarming, and the awful discovery is made that when the rewind knob is turned nothing happens! A sign that something must have gone wrong inside the camera!

This happened to me once on a mountain tour where, needless to say, there was no darkroom within miles around. The film had been torn from its cassette, and it was lying open inside the camera. In order to insert a new one, I had to sacrifice it, throwing it with a deep sigh over the yawning precipice. The day was too glorious to miss the opportunity of further pictures.

Helpful changing bag

For such cases we could with advantage take a changing bag along and operate inside its "sleeve". Rubber bands keep its entrance so tight, that with practised fingers we could repair the damage in the absolute darkness of this portable darkroom, while the rest of our body stays outside. Incidentally the black bag can also be put to excellent use as neutral background for close-up pictures such as flowers.

However, I am afraid you will have left this handy gimmick at home just when it will be most urgently needed. In an emergency you may perhaps ask your traveling companion (the word "fellow traveler" having a somewhat ambiguous ring these days) to lock you into a big wardrobe after the room has been blacked out. Or – but this is a question of breathing technique – you could crawl under a heavy blanket, which is then tucked in around you on all sides. I have been through all this!

Thank heavens it happens only very rarely that the color film is torn from the cassette spool. If it does happen, I can only wish it will be after the last exposure of a sunset. The night will be your most efficient darkroom!

Be Nice to Each Other!

A tired extra in a film studio once told me that there are two kinds of film directors – good ones, and rude ones. At least this is how the actors see them. The rude ones rant and rave, and their spirit rapidly percolates through the whole studio down to the humblest lighting technician. And finally, the result of the general ill-temper comes home to roost with the impatient boss.

We amateurs, too, can learn a little from this example. Patience is a virtue benefiting photography in general – restlessness and hurry are often the culprits if the wrong lighting and faulty composition spoil an originally attractive subject.

Human beings, too, need to be treated with patience, even if they are members of your own family and your own children! They often serve – photographically speaking – as your models. And they have to, whether they happen to be in the mood for it or not!

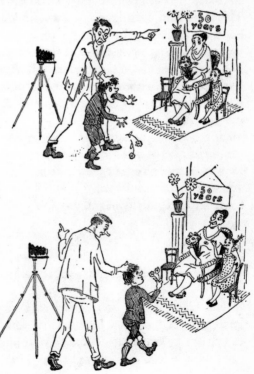

If they are not, the photograph will betray it at once! They just refuse to "play ball" merely taking up their positions as ordered. One can really sense the compulsion, the "I don't want to, but I have to"!

Be nice to each other, then, always, if you can, and not only when you need friendly faces. The friendliness and high spirits of models who enjoy the whole procedure can inspire the amateur behind the camera. Good humour improves the pictures immensely; if you are in a bad mood, you had far better leave your camera alone.

Be nice also to the incidental models that you meet here and there. The good-natured stall-holder – perhaps you might buy a pound of apples from her before you "shoot" her – or the peasant behind his plough – a few friendly words, perhaps no more than a remark about the weather – will be enough to establish human contact.

Legal aspects

Some people do not want to have their photographs taken. Some even refuse it outright. Perhaps you are not aware of this "right to one's own picture" which exists in some continental countries. If, for instance, you publish a photograph showing a person who has refused permission for it, you may cause yourself a lot of trouble. Generally you must obtain the express consent of the person shown. Particularly, of course, if such a picture is to be used for advertising purposes.

There are subtle distinctions, though. A personality such as a well-known politician or artist in the centre of public interest cannot take you to court, no matter how unflattering the circumstances in which hou have taken his picture (unless he is shown in an offensive manner). But Mrs. Jones with her shopping bag on her arm, of whom you took a snap when she was having a peaceful chat with her neighbour, can sue you for damages. Her claim would certainly be successful if the picture were to be used for advertising, and she was made to recommend a certain brand of detergent washing "whiter than white".

However, enough of our pseudo-legal discourse. All I wanted to say to you was that friendliness, if it is not merely put on, but comes from the heart, generally opens all doors to you.

Calmness, the photographer's first need

Let me tell you, finally, that hustle and bustle are definitely detrimental to good photography, apart perhaps from unrepeatable snapshots.

If you have become accustomed to a certain procedure for taking your pictures, you will benefit from this when the need arises. For example: – take the camera out of your pocket, or open the ever ready case, remove lens cap (always slide it into the same trouser pocket),

192

measure exposure, set stop and exposure time – raise camera to your eye, check picture area, measure the range. This would be my own sequence. And never hurry!

Again, being hustled either by your watch or by other people is fatal. You must take your time and ignore other people. Sometimes they can even be educated, once they have come to realize that there is a difference between "snapshooting" and "taking photographs".

Some Words about the Transparency

Color transparencies in cardboard frames

They are called slides in the States, where every transparency is mounted singly in a cardboard frame. Special machines in the developing stations cut the transparencies precisely, and nimble girls' fingers in silk gloves do the mounting in frames. Naturally, this piece-work method precludes any accurate alignment of the pictures or any improvement of the picture area. Moreover, in its cardboard frame the transparency is exposed to scratches and dirt.

These slides are very convenient so long as they are merely examined in a viewing device (it is a pity that the manufacturers of the many models of slide viewers have not yet found a way of illuminating the transparencies with bright white light. In most of them the light is far too yellow.)

I prefer the viewers without special light source. Either the viewer is held against the sunlit window sill or a bright incandescent lamp screened with thin, white paper.

Cardboard Mounts or Glass?

Cardboard slides, at any rate, allow a quick sorting out for quality: into the best, the good, and the not-so-good. The best are of course kept in a special box, the merely acceptable ones are held in reserve, and what you do with your duds is your own affair. I get rid of the throwouts as quickly as possible, even going to the length of burning mine so that the dustman cannot see the rubbish I produced with my camera.

Cardboard mounts would be wonderful if they did not soon begin to pop during projection. They buckle, and each slide must then be re-focused after a few seconds. Thereafter, the cardboard slide will be projected sharply even during prolonged periods, and with projection lenses of short focal lengths they will appear wholly sharp from corner to corner while difficulties are experienced with long focal lengths. Also, a cardboard slide is less subject to heating during projection than one mounted between glass, a fact which I found out only recently.

However, the buckles forming in the glassless slide during prolonged projection will in time become chronic, and if the precious work of art is mounted between glass at some later stage it will become apparent that the film can no longer be brought into the ideal focusing plane, with the immediate occurence of the dread Newton's rings.

In my experience, cardboard-mounted slides can be projected for short periods without any risk. But you should decide quickly which are to be glass-mounted, and favor this method in the interest of your best pictures.

Masking of Disturbing Details Along the Picture Margins

Hence, if you love your slides you mount them between glass. Maybe your photo-dealer will relieve you of this job, but it would be better if you did it yourself, because you will then be able, by masking the picture area, to improve them considerably even at this stage. The usual black and white masks are a little smaller than the 24 × 36 mm. color picture and enable you at least to correct a slanting horizon. Also, most disturbing details along the margin which are not part of the pictorial content can be masked off with success.

It is important for these masks to be very neatly stamped out without any fibers and loose particles protruding into the picture during projection.

Often you will want to shorten the long or the short dimension of your slide. This is done by masking with the black adhesive strip used for binding the glass-slides, or with parts of the preset mask itself, whose black paper, cut into narrow strips, is an excellent means for masking off unwanted parts of the picture. To make them stick it is enough to moisten them slightly where they do not come into contact with the slide itself, so that in the case of errors the mask can be removed again without damage to the slide.

Prefabricated Slide Frames

There are innumerable slide frames on the market, designed to make slide mounting easier; some of them even permit the removal of the piece of film as from a cassette, so that it can be replaced by another. However, this impairs the freedom from dust which in the long run can only be guaranteed if the glass slide is sealed tightly all round. This guarantee is really assured only by the simplest method using two 2 × 2" glass plates and black binding strip. If you apply as little moisture as possible for binding your slide will remain dry and give you nothing but joy whenever you project it. You will soon be given further details about the procedure of glass mounting.

Trouble with Newton's rings

Newton's rings are peculiar features displaying all colors of the rainbow on a glass-mounted transparency. During projection they often writhe in fantastic shapes, arousing the profound interest of the viewers, but disturbing the pictorial impression.

We all know that these colored rings are caused by the glossy back of the film coming too close to the cover glass. Normally a little space remains between film and cover glass due to the mask protecting the little transparency. This is as it should be, because it prevents the ideally plane film from coming into direct or indirect contact with the glass. However, if the film has been previously subjected to stress or was not bone dry during mounting, such contact and the resulting disturbance of Newton's rings becomes possible and even likely.

A further spacing mask will sometimes cure this if it is placed over the glossy side of the affected transparencies. But it will not help in stubborn cases.

An entirely new remedy for Newton's rings

Perhaps you know already that the condenser lenses of the Leitz enlargers are chemically treated, so that their plane surfaces are specially roughened. This has the purpose of avoiding the formation of Newton's rings without in any way affecting the plane position of the film.

The same roughening process has been applied to transparency cover glasses, of course in an extremely mild form. The treated glasses are a little more expensive than untreated 2 × 2 inch glasses.

Now it is by no means necessary to mount all transparencies, and both sides at that, between these specially prepared Newlo transparency cover glasses. It is quite sufficient to use one on the glossy side only, and a normal cover glass is used to cover the emulsion side.

My first experiments have shown that in more than 75 % of all cases the removal of the disturbing color rings is possible. It would, therefore, perhaps be a good idea to lay in a small stock of Newlo glasses for use where Newton's rings do occur.

196

Per-O-Color frames

There are large numbers of transparency frames on the market, in order to make mounting easier for the amateur. Among them, the Per-O-Color frames, made in Switzerland under licence from Leitz, occupy a special position in that their design guarantees almost complete freedom from dust and a plane position of the color transparency. Their detailed description here would be going too far. However, since I began to use these frames for my lectures, trouble with re-focusing has considerably diminished. The tendency of Newton's rings is prevented by extremely thin masks. Where they did occur nevertheless, I got rid of them with the specially treated Newlo glasses. It is well worth your while to look at these Per-O-Color frames at your photo dealer.

"Why are your transparencies so clean?"

Due to its frequency, this question takes pride of place among all questions put to me after every one of my slide lectures. Well, the comparison is not altogether a fair one. Dust and other troubles are noticed far more easily with a small picture and a short projection distances at home than if one looks at transparencies on a large screen at the appropriate viewing distance.

But I do admit that I take great pains with the glass mounting of my good color transparencies. I would like to list the most important aids in the battle against dust: –

1) the developed color film should be stored free from dust as much as possible, i.e. in the bags from the processing station. Single, already-cut color transparencies should be kept in small envelopes or between sheets of paper.

2) as soon as the transparencies have been placed in their self-sealing mask, they should not be left lying about, but kept in envelopes or stacked in a box, so that they cannot be damaged by scratches.

3) the cover glasses must be cleaned even if the makers claim them to be clean.
   Cleaning is made easier by the use of some quick-drying window cleaning agent and polishing with a clean piece of linen. This is a matter of seconds.

4) Now we enter the decisive stage. The clean cover glass is held against a dark background, so that the surface of the glass shows up every particle of dust. If this cannot be removed simply by blowing it away, it should be got rid of gently with a broad sable brush. As soon as the cover glass is obviously free from dust, replace it quickly on the transparency, which had also been examined for the absence of dust. The same routine is quickly followed with the second glass – finished!

Finished? Maybe! At least I hope so. But it could just happen that another dust gremlin is discovered which, in spite of all precautions, has found its way to film or glass at the last moment. This sets the whole rigmarole going again from the start – a photo-technical version of "snakes and ladders".

However, I do it in a way more exciting than it needs to be in practice. I am now going to tell you a little secret, which makes the whole job considerably easier for me. As we all know, dust particles in the transparency will only be noticeable if they become lodged on uniformly bright and large portions of the picture, especially in the sky! However, not all transparencies show any sky or large, white fronts of buildings. I would even say that the majority of transparencies will stand being mounted with a little dust without harm.

Such subjects are night scenes, autumn woods, street scenes without sky, group pictures – the possibilities are far too many to be mentioned here. Among every hundred of my transparencies there are at least twenty-five that could be described as "dust sensitive", and I organize my work accordingly. Either I mount the "problem children" first, a puzzle game which is time-consuming, or I save them up to the end. The others will be finished all the quicker for it.

Far be it for me to advise you to proceed in a slap-dash manner here. But at least you can save yourself hunting for every single bit of dust.

Anti-static agents

For dust detectives amongst amateurs I have the following tip: In America they sell a fine sable brush under the name of Staticmaster, and similar brushes are now available in Britain and Europe. With a single stroke it neutralizes the static charge of films. In fact, every piece of film is only too anxious to act as a magnet for dust. If, for instance, a piece of film is rubbed with a piece of cloth and held, just for fun, over an ashtray, the volatile particles of ash rise, as if lifted by a magic hand, upwards and adhere to the film. It possesses a static charge – proof of its attraction for dust. The Staticmaster acts as it were, as a vacuum cleaner in miniature.

The considerably cheaper cloths also available have similar antistatic properties. The Faber anti-static cloth is one of them.

Every film rubbed with this cloth loses its inclination to attract dust. This is obviously particularly useful for black-and-white films before they are placed in the enlarger.

Marking strips

The further treatment of your transparencies, at long last mounted under glass and bound with adhesive tape, is entirely up to you. Whether you fix the white marking strip across the top or the bottom is a matter of custom. It is convenient to place it at the foot of the picture, so that one sees at once during projection which is the top and which the bottom. Two or three transparencies shown upside down during a lecture may cause a certain amount of merriment, but just as no joke should be repeated too often, this should not happen too frequently either.

There is yet another trick I want to tell you. The finished transparencies can be filed in boxes or any type of container, where they should be arranged with their white edges facing the top. I, therefore, make a rule of putting the white strip across the bottom margin of the picture. Thus all I have to do is take them out and insert them in the same position (upside down) in the projector. However, how do you know whether the transparency is projected right-way-round or laterally reversed? True, normally we find a white and a dark side on the strip. The white one is inserted so that it faces the lamp. However, if all the transparencies are filed together in one box, order can be established once and for all with a single sweep of the hand. The correctly filed transparencies are marked along the right-hand third or the right-hand corner with a grease pencil (red, green, or any other color) by quickly drawing it across the row of slides.

If a picture thus marked finds its way into the box right-way-up, but wrong way round, it will at once be recognized as an "outsider". Obviously this grease pencil system can also be extended. With four different colors in all possible combinations, hundreds of variants can be obtained for one's transparencies according to their subject. There are no limits to your imagination.

Durability of color films

I think I can answer the question whether your grandchildren will get the same enjoyment from your glass-mounted transparencies as you do with "yes" – provided you store them in a dry place.

Many a veteran color amateur has unfortunately discovered the truth of this from the evidence of transparencies which did not survive storage in a damp cellar. Their colors turned more or less into a purplish pink. I know that to-day more stable dye substances preserve color film. At any rate, I can now look back on approximately six years' post-war experience. Some slides have been projected more than 400 times, but no color changes have yet taken place!

Exposed films should be developed soon!

The one tip with only an indirect bearing in this context continues to be valid.

Color films still have expiration dates which should not be exceeded.

If it does happen, the film can naturally still be used, but it had better be set aside for those subjects which are repeatable.

However, there is no guarantee if we take some pictures, then leave the camera with the partly exposed film lying about for months before using up the rest of the film. This can happen quite inadvertently, but you must not be surprised if the most recently exposed pictures show the better color rendering. This fading of the undeveloped image does not happen after days or weeks, but a delay of months is a more serious matter. If we keep this in mind, we will avoid unpleasant surprises.

There is a general rule that exposed films should not wait longer than six weeks for development. Here, too, the method of storage plays a certain part.

Many a rumour has been heard about the keeping qualities of unexposed and exposed films in the tropics. Conditions there vary widely. The regions with the prefix "sub" are by far the more dangerous for the film. It dislikes sudden temperature changes as much as humidity. Landlubbers cannot imagine the damage wrought by humidity. If you live on the coast you will know what I mean. And if you live in the subtropics your experiences will be enough to make other people's hair stand on end.

The simplest method of keeping film dry is a tin with a well-closing lid sealed and air-tight all round. Inside, in addition to the film, a few handfuls of rice, which attracts moisture. Another remedy which can be bought in any chemist's shop is Silica-gel.

My Dear Friends,

I already told you elsewhere that it is hardly possible to cram into this book everything that can be said about color photography without expanding it into a veritable tome, a photographic encyclopedia as it were.

All the same, my conscience is not unduly disturbed as I now say good-by to you. I know that you are by now familiar with the basic principles of color photography, and that you can carry on under your own steam.

If you have come unstuck and in spite of careful study are at your wits' end I will only be too pleased to help you further along. Do not hesitate to let me have your questions through the publishers. But please don't be cross if you have to wait a little for my answer, because I am often away on my lecture tours where I meet my friends, the photo-fans.

It would be nice if we were to meet there one day – your pictures and your questions will be welcome!

Yours sincerely

Walther Benser

202